# The Judgement of History

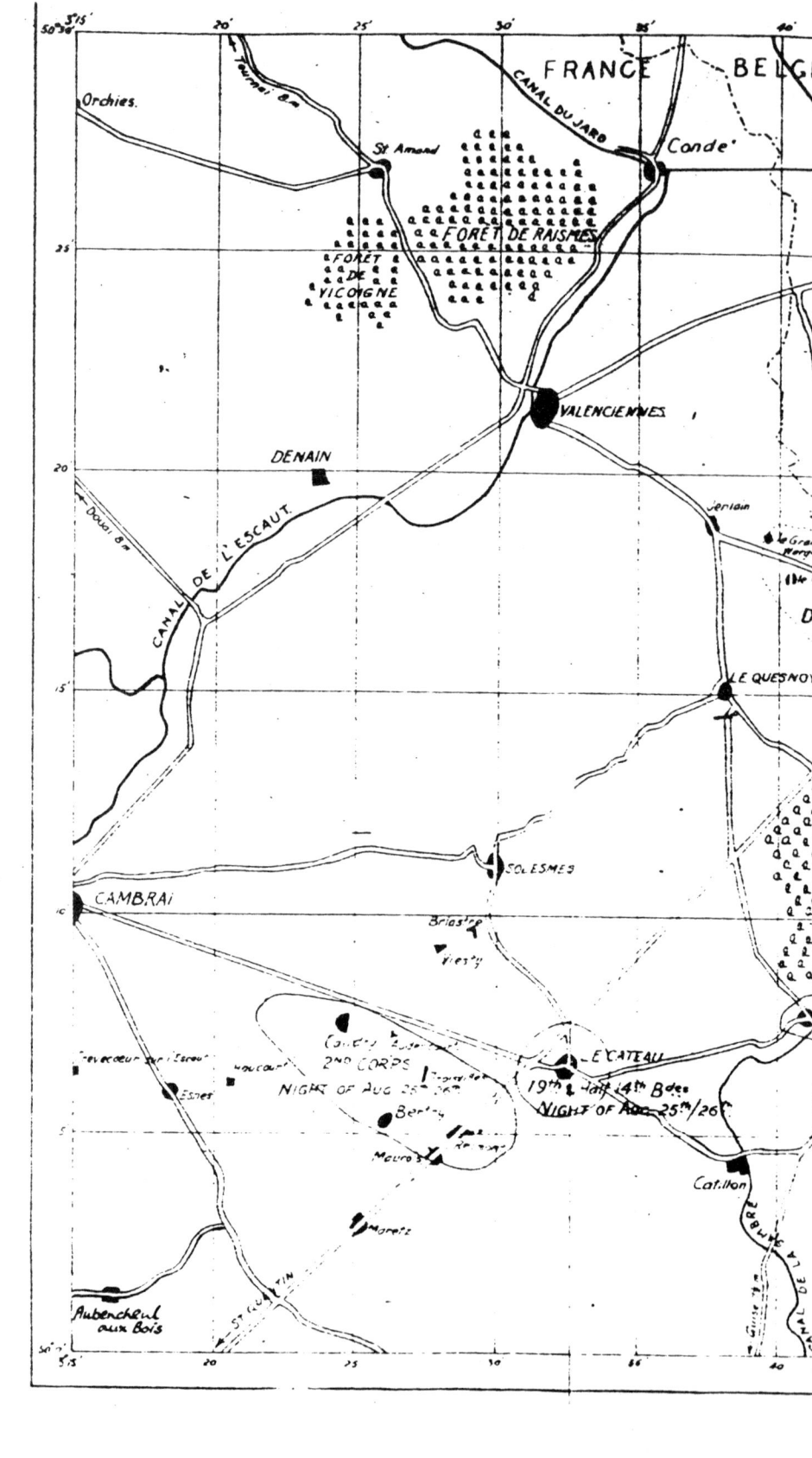

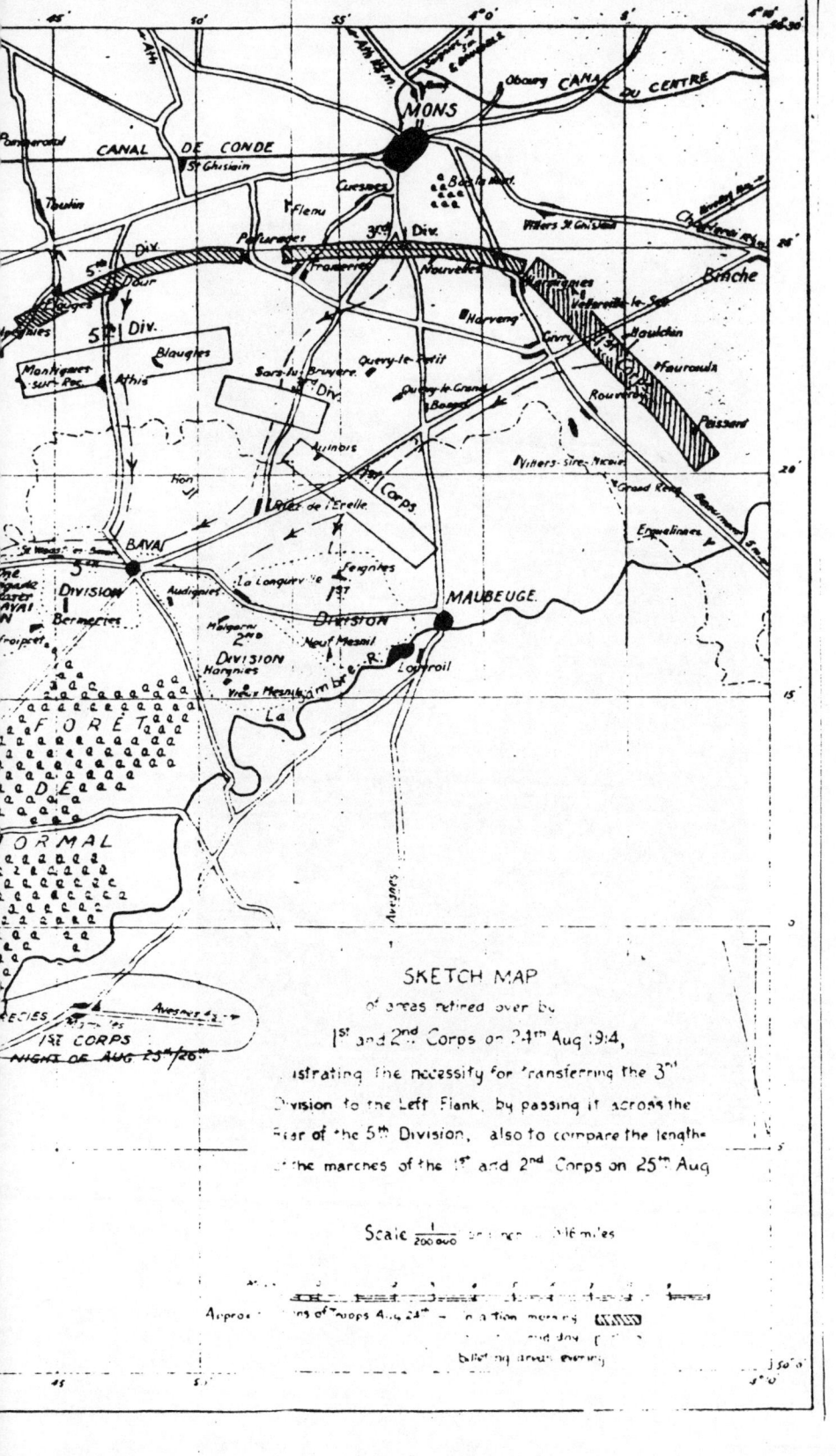

# THE JUDGEMENT OF HISTORY
Sir Horace Smith Dorrien, Lord French and 1914

Incorporating General Smith-Dorrien's Statement with regard to Lord French's book *1914*, with an introductory essay by

Dr. Ian F.W. Beckett

Tom Donovan
London

First published in 1993 by

Tom Donovan Publishing Ltd.
52 Willow Road
Hampstead
London NW3 1TP

©1993 Ian F.W.Beckett & Tom Donovan Publishing Ltd.

ISBN (Hardback) 1-871085-14-4
ISBN (Paperback) 1-871085-15-2

All rights reserved. No part of this publication may be reproduced, stored in a retrieval system or transmitted in any form, by any means, electrical, mechanical or otherwise, without first seeking the written permission of the copyright owner and of the publisher.

Desk-top typeset by Tom Donovan Publishing Ltd.

Printed in Great Britain by
Antony Rowe Ltd, Chippenham, Wiltshire

# Contents

General Sir Horace Smith-Dorrien     vi
Introduction     vii

The complete text of General Sir Horace Smith-Dorrien's *Statement with regard to the first edition of Lord French's book "1914"* appears after page xxvi. It includes minor ink corrections in the author's own hand.

The sketch map of the actions of Mons and Le Cateau which appears at the front of this book originally folded out at the end of the *Statement*. It has been reduced in order to accomodate it.

# General Smith-Dorrien

General Sir Horace Smith-Dorrien was born on 26 May 1858 at Haresfoot, Berkhamstead, a soldier's son and the eleventh of fifteen children. Educated at Harrow, he entered the Royal Military College, Sandhurst in February 1876 and was commissioned in the 2nd Battalion, Sherwood Foresters (95th Foot). After service in Ireland he proceeded on special service to South Africa for the Zulu campaign of 1879 and, while undertaking transport duties, was among the few regular officers to escape from the field of Isandhlwana. Further service followed in Ireland, Egypt during the 1882 campaign and India before Smith-Dorrien was seconded to the Egyptian Army during the Suakin campaign. He studied at the Staff College, Camberley from 1887 to 1889 and saw further active service during the Tirah campaign on the North West Frontier in 1897 and as commander of a Sudanese battalion in the Sudan campaign of 1898. He was commanding the Sherwood Foresters at the outbreak of the South African War in 1899 but received command of the 19th Brigade in February 1900 and was soon afterwards promoted to Major-General. After distinguishing himself in command of a column during the latter stages of the war on the veldt he went to India as Adjutant-General from 1902 to 1903 and then commanded the 4th Division of the Indian Army from 1903 to 1905. The prestigious Aldershot Command came to Smith-Dorrien in 1907 followed by a stint in Southern Command in 1911. A full general since 1912, Smith-Dorrien was still at Southern Command when war broke out in August 1914. Sent to command II Corps upon the death of Sir James Grierson, Smith-Dorrien became commander of the Second Army in December 1914. Resigning his command in May 1915 he was then designated Commander-in-Chief in East Africa but was compelled through ill-health to return to England before actually assuming command in the field in early 1916. He became Governor of Gibraltar in 1918, retiring from the army in September 1923. He died on 12 August 1930 as a result of injuries sustained in a road accident. Just 28 copies of General Sir Horace Smith-Dorrien's *Statement with regard to the first edition of Lord French's book, '1914'* were privately circulated in December 1919.

# Introduction

In April 1919 the *Daily Telegraph* began serialising extracts from Field Marshal Viscount French's forthcoming memoir, *1914*, the book itself being published two months later. Effectively the first such memoir by any leading participant in the conduct of the Great War, it was not perhaps unexpected to find *The Times Literary Supplement* declaring it the most illuminating document yet published on the war.[1] Heightening the impact of French's book, which had been largely compiled by a journalist on *The Times*, Lovat Fraser, from conversations with the field marshal,[2] was the seeming candour of one who was still serving as Lord Lieutenant of Ireland, in revealing wartime disputes at the highest levels of policy-making. It was also remarkable for the vigour with which French attacked the reputations of real or imagined enemies. The late Secretary of State for War, Field Marshal Earl Kitchener, was a principal target of *1914* and, more indirectly, so was the former prime minister, Asquith. Some of the most extreme of French's statements, however, were reserved for his former corps and army commander, General Sir Horace Smith-Dorrien, who was also still serving, as Governor of Gibraltar.

French's book raised the serious question of the degree to which policy-makers should or could be restricted from publishing matters which might be regarded as subject to the somewhat indistinct interpretation of what constituted official secrecy. In the event, *1914* proved only a starting point to the even greater threat posed by subsequent memoirs with new rules evolving only gradually between 1919 and 1934. Nevertheless, its appearance presented a particular difficulty for a man such as Smith-Dorrien, who was widely regarded as too upright a man 'with far too fine a sense of discipline to enter into controversy.' In fact there were soldiers either genuinely diffident towards their own reputations or who chose deliberately to keep their silence in the post-war 'battle of the memoirs,'[3] but Smith-Dorrien was not to be numbered among them. Without actually appearing to enter the lists, he found means to circumvent the restrictions placed upon him and, indeed, was to prove more successful than many of his contemporaries - not least French - in securing a favourable judgement for posterity.

\* \* \*

# I

As is well known, Smith-Dorrien was sent out by Kitchener to command II Corps when Lieutenant-General Sir James Grierson suffered a fatal heart attack on 17 August 1914 en route for the British Expeditionary Force's concentration area, despite French having specifically requested that Sir Herbert Plumer be appointed. It was common knowledge that, although once friends, French and Smith-Dorrien were on the worst possible personal terms, the quarrel apparently dating back to 1909 when, having succeeded the cavalryman French in the premier Aldershot command two years earlier, the infantryman Smith-Dorrien had taken a highly critical view of the traditional role of the *arme blanche*. It was also suggested later that its beginning was marked by French's unfair criticism of Smith-Dorrien at that year's autumn manoeuvres.[4] Admittedly, Smith-Dorrien had a notoriously violent temper seemingly linked to sudden attacks of neuralgia, but he was a highly capable soldier whose tenure at Aldershot was marked by innovative practicality. Arriving in France on 20 August without any knowledge of the pre-war mobilisation plans and finding a corps whose units were unfamiliar with each other and a largely improvised staff,[5] Smith-Dorrien was soon plunged into the chaos of the Expeditionary Force's retreat before the superior numbers of General Alexander von Kluck's advancing German First Army.

As it happened, Smith-Dorrien's relationship with the I Corps commander, Sir Douglas Haig, was scarcely better than that with his commander-in-chief, French, while his chief of staff, Brigadier-General George Forestier-Walker, was on equally bad terms with Haig's chief of staff, Brigadier-General John Gough.[6] As the two corps retreated from the first engagement at Mons on 23 August and with French and his staff failing to exercise proper control, their paths rapidly diverged on either side of the forest of Mormal, with all contact lost between 26 August and 1 September. Having suffered by far the greater number of casualties at Mons and being far more closely pressed than Haig, Smith-Dorrien then took the decision to stand at Le Cateau on 26 August in spite of French's orders to continue to retreat. At some cost, Smith-Dorrien delivered a sharp jolt to his German pursuers and undoubtedly saved the Expeditionary Force as a whole, a fact subsequently acknowledged by French in his official campaign despatch of 7 September 1914, wherein Smith-Dorrien's 'rare and unusual coolness, intrepidity and determination' were duly praised. French made similar remarks on other occasions that September and,

## Introduction

during November 1914, Smith-Dorrien was also lavish in his public approbation for French's handling of the first battle of Ypres.[7] In reality, relations remained distinctly cool and then deteriorated further through the spring of 1915. His command having been translated into Second Army in December 1914, Smith-Dorrien had all troops removed from his control on 30 April 1915 for alleged pessimism during the second battle of Ypres and on 6 May he resigned.

In fact, there had already been one brief precursor of the future controversy in February 1917, the *Weekly Despatch* having published a report of an interview with Smith-Dorrien - actually conducted by telephone - in which he explained his decision to stand at Le Cateau. At that time French had set Lovat Fraser to work on his behalf to repudiate Smith-Dorrien's version of events, the latter always attributing the hostility shown him in *1914* to the interview. While the subsequent dismissal of Smith-Dorrien was not addressed in *1914*, French now claimed that his despatch of September 1914 had been written hurriedly and before the full facts were known. Le Cateau had become an unnecessary action costing 14,000 casualties and the loss of 80 guns fought by a corps well capable of continuing the retreat and a commander prone to pessimism and depression. Indeed, at a conference of senior officers at Compiegne on 29 August Smith-Dorrien had offered only a 'counsel of despair' in suggesting that the expeditionary force should 'retire to our base, thoroughly refit, re-embark, and try to land at some favourable point on the coast line.' The same pessimism had also marked Smith-Dorrien's conduct during the first battle of Ypres in the autumn of 1914.[8]

In defence of publication while technically a serving soldier, since field marshals may not be deemed to have retired, French was to claim that he was not occupying the office of Lord Lieutenant in his military capacity. Indeed, it was a political appointment, but French frequently wore uniform and had once described himself as a 'military viceroy.' However, while stating that French's book would not be defended if the matter were raised at Westminster, Andrew Bonar Law, who was acting as prime minister in Lloyd George's absence at the Paris peace conference, indicated that French would not be compelled to resign unless members of Parliament demanded it.[9] For Smith-Dorrien, however, a different policy was to prevail, his request that he be allowed to reply to French's charges - as outlined in the extracts appearing in the *Daily Telegraph* he had read - being sent to the War

Office from Gibraltar on 14 May 1919 following a personal appeal to the Secretary of State for War, Viscount Milner, six days earlier. With further extracts being published, Smith-Dorrien again wrote on 5 June requesting that a royal commission be convened to examine all the relevant records, once more copying his request to Milner, who had replied to Smith-Dorrien's original communication on 24 May suggesting a formal approach to the Army Council, in apparent ignorance of the letter already sent to the War Office.

With no apparent sense of irony, that most politically active of soldiers, Sir Henry Wilson, now Chief of the Imperial General Staff, advised the Secretary of State to prevent any public reply by Smith-Dorrien 'because if we once allow officers on full pay to get writing to newspapers it seems to me there will be no end to the amount of damage it will do to the army...' Accordingly, on 21 June the War Office replied to Smith-Dorrien that he could not be allowed the right of public reply while on the active list 'in the interests of discipline' and also rejecting any royal commission. However, Smith-Dorrien would be permitted to place his view of events in 1914 on the record for internal consumption. Finding the official equivocation over French's precise military status particularly irksome, Smith-Dorrien claimed that it would be in the interest of the service to allow reply, but elicited no further response. Clearly his reputation must be served by those means available to him. There seems little reason to doubt that Smith-Dorrien had not previously intended to become involved in any controversies. As he had written to Milner on 5 June, 'Although I knew I had been most unfairly treated in France, I had made up my mind, rather than injure Lord French's reputation, merely to leave a memoir for my children, never to be published whilst he or I were alive. Silence has now become impossible.'[11]

## II

To a large extent, Smith-Dorrien was already advantaged by the sensation surrounding the serialisation of French's book and he was well aware that 'in trying to wipe me out [French] has given me the chance of re-establishing my reputation, whilst killing himself.' Of French's literary efforts *The Times* remarked in June 1919 that 'No book of modern times has been so extensively discussed in advance of its appearance' although it also chose to take a generally benevolent view of French's motives. Asquith quickly spoke in defence of his

## Introduction

administration's munitions policy, which alone among post-1914 events had been covered in French's last chapter, at London's Connaught Rooms on 3 June and rushed his speech into print as *The Great Shell Story*. Similarly, Major-General Sir Charles Callwell sprang to the defence of Kitchener in a review article in *The Morning Post*.[12]

An even more savage riposte to *1914*, however, was the review by the Honorable J.W. (later Sir John) Fortescue in the October 1919 issue of *The Quarterly Review*. The Royal Librarian and a distinguished military historian, Fortescue had reluctantly accepted appointment as an official historian in February 1916 and had since laboured on an account of operations on the Western Front up to May 1915 under increasingly restrictive official conditions. In fact, Fortescue had already declared *1914* 'as remarkable for its omissions as for its obvious contradictions and misstatements' in a piece for *The Observer* in June, but the review in October went even further in proclaiming the book 'one of the most unfortunate ever written' with 'misstatements and misrepresentations of the most ludicrous kind' proving French manifestly unfit to be regarded in the same company as the great British soldiers of the past. Indeed, Fortescue was later to write in *Blackwood's Magazine* of his first reaction to *1914*: "After a very short perusal I fell back aghast, saying the 'The man must be mad.'" His most charitable conclusion was that it was 'the work of a monomaniac.'[13]

Fortescue was promptly dismissed as an official historian for his 'partiality' in the matter of French and it was the case that his attitude towards *1914* was not wholly disinterested. Not only had Fortescue's brother been dismissed from command of 80th Brigade in 27th Division by French in March 1915 but Fortescue was also an old friend of Smith-Dorrien, whom he had first known as a schoolboy at Harrow. There does not appear to have been any correspondence between the two during 1919, although Fortescue was to receive a copy of Smith-Dorrien's wartime journal from the King's assistant private secretary in November. Similarly, in December Fortescue received a copy of the privately circulated *Statement*, reproduced here, refuting French's allegations, which Smith-Dorrien was to prepare at the same time as that permitted by the War Office. Fortescue was also involved in the deposit of a copy of the latter in the British Museum in 1923.

Nonetheless, it is highly likely that Fortescue had previously discussed the 1914 campaign with Smith-Dorrien in the interval between the latter returning ill from the Cape in 1916 - whence he had gone en route to take command of the campaign in German East Africa - and departing for Gibraltar in September 1918. Certainly, Smith-Dorrien had written to congratulate Fortescue on the latest volume of his monumental *A History of the British Army* in the autumn of 1917. Fortescue had also rewritten his account of Le Cateau twice, the first revision occasioned by the return of some prisoners of war in November 1917 and the second after the 'belated discovery' of new but unspecified documents in January 1919.[14]

Fortescue was therefore an important ally and by no means the only author who could be relied upon, since it would appear that, in common with Haig, a conscious aspect of Smith-Dorrien's campaign of justification was to assist in the preparation of others' accounts of events which would serve his own purposes. Thus, Sir Henry Newbolt, who would be employed as an official naval historian in a similar way to Fortescue for the army, was another acquaintance whose *Tales of the Great War* was highly favourable to Smith-Dorrien. Newbolt also possessed a copy of Smith-Dorrien's wartime journal and, in giving Smith-Dorrien some warning in February 1919 of what he had learned of French's likely charges, undertook to write to the press himself although advising Smith-Dorrien to 'keep a dignified silence' for the time being. Naturally, Newbolt also received a copy of Smith-Dorrien's private statement in December 1919.[15]

In March 1919 Newbolt sent a copy of Major-General Sir Frederick Maurice's *Forty Days in 1914*, which although primarily recounting the campaign from the point of view of the Germans, was 'impartial' in its references to Smith-Dorrien's part in the campaign. Maurice had his own campaign to wage with respect to the termination of his military career in May 1918 and his book on the 1914 campaign was partially intended to derive lessons for the higher direction of war from the German experience. However, he did conclude of Le Cateau that Smith-Dorrien's 'courage in accepting battle had been justified.'[16] Smith-Dorrien's attention having thus been drawn to the book, he soon obtained a copy and sent his congratulations to Maurice in June 1919. Maurice, who had served on the staff of 3rd Division in II Corps during the campaign, was a useful witness to the thoughts of his divisional commander, Hubert Hamilton, who had been killed in October 1914 and, shortly after first corresponding with Smith-Dorrien, found his own mislaid diary of the retreat. Maurice was also familiar with German sources, not least the memoir being prepared by von Kluck,

Introduction                                                                 xiii

with whom he was in correspondence, and in November 1919 he published his own critical review of *1914* in the *National Review*. Subsequently, the bibliography of the second edition of Maurice's book in 1920 offered both this review and that by Fortescue, with whom Maurice was also in contact, as correctives to French's version of events.[17]

Smith-Dorrien was also in correspondence with Edgar Wallace only for the latter to give up his attempt to write a history of the 1914 campaign in July 1919 because he felt that not enough material was yet available to do so. However, other published accounts did uphold Smith-Dorrien's reputation. In fact, the first had been as early as September 1916, Major A. Corbett-Smith's *The Retreat from Mons* emphasising French's praise of Smith-Dorrien in the official despatch of September 1914, which was reproduced as an appendix, and claiming that the country owed the II Corps commander 'an imperishable debt.' Corbett-Smith had served under Smith-Dorrien before the war as well as during the campaign itself and acknowledged the general's assistance in providing information and 'reading the proof sheets.' French, under whom Corbett-Smith was then serving as a battery commander, was particularly suspicious of the circumstances surrounding the book, which had been reprinted four times by November 1916, and this undoubtedly contributed to his reaction to Smith-Dorrien's interview with *The Weekly Despatch* a few months later. Corbett-Smith was not alone in utilising French's own despatch, for its reference to Smith-Dorrien was also highlighted in another immensely popular wartime publication, Lord Ernest Hamilton's *The First Seven Divisions*, which went through fourteen impressions in 1916.

Smith-Dorrien had been in contact with Corbett-Smith but this was not the case with Hamilton or with another artilleryman, Major A.F.Becke, whose *The Royal Artillery at Le Cateau* appearing in January 1919 took a similarly favourable view of Smith-Dorrien's generalship. Primarily designed to demonstrate the use to which surviving war diaries might be put and to encourage officers to supplement official documents with personal testimony, Becke's account suggested that Le Cateau was both a 'triumph' and 'one of the most important delaying actions recorded in history.'[18]

## III

Becke was already attached to the military history branch of the Historical Section of the Committee of Imperial Defence at the time he wrote his book, hence the emphasis upon getting officers to send in additional information. Thus, he was to figure in the second principal means by which Smith-Dorrien advanced his cause, namely the preparation of the statement which the War Office had authorised and the effort to influence the conclusions of the Official History. Smith-Dorrien originally approached Becke with regard to his access to war diaries and Becke was then charged by the head of the branch, Brigadier-General (later Sir) James Edmonds, with providing Smith-Dorrien with facts and figures from official records since Smith-Dorrien could clearly not consult them in person from Gibraltar. Becke was also to work on the first volume of the Official History, covering Mons and Le Cateau, which was published in 1923.

In fact, the preparation of both the *Summary of Mis-statements* in French's book for the War Office and also the longer memorandum prepared simultaneously for private circulation, General Sir Horace Smith-Dorrien's *Statement with regard to the first edition of Lord French's book, 1914* which is reproduced here, were not the first occasion on which Smith-Dorrien had sought to place his version of events on record. In May 1915 he had prepared a memorandum on his resignation for War Office files, which was reproduced in the later *Statement*. Moreover, during his period of command, in addition to his diary, he had written a daily journal to be forwarded to the King. The request for such a journal had emanated from the King, with whom Smith-Dorrien had been on close terms for many years. It was by no means unusual for the King to make such a request and Smith-Dorrien had also been asked to forward regular accounts of his then command's activities in 1911. Smith-Dorrien had made no secret of the King's request when first arriving at French's headquarters on 20 August 1914. In fact, the King had specifically instructed him to seek French's permission, a point which was made perfectly clear in a slight revision to the wording of the original text of Smith-Dorrien's longer personal statement sought by the King's assistant secretary, Clive Wigram, in January 1920. Smith-Dorrien's adherence to the sovereign's wishes was evident to all and those letters received from the King's private secretary, Lord Stamfordham, or Wigram, were invariably circulated by Smith-Dorrien among his staff. Some extracts from the journal

## Introduction

prepared for the King may also have gone to Kitchener or the Army Council since Smith-Dorrien asked Wigram in September 1914 if he would be willing to make copies for them.[19]

In 1919 the King was especially disturbed by French's book, Wigram writing to Smith-Dorrien of its 'un-English and ungenerous' nature and, in fact, French was to have 'a chilly audience' at the palace on 9 May. Clearly, the King did not wish to see what Wigram expressed to French as any 'discordant note sounded by angry disputes and personal wrangling,' especially when the war was not technically over. Equally, however, Wigram was anxious to pursuade Smith-Dorrien that, in view of French's literary excesses, 'public opinion' would prove of greater value than some costly royal commission in vindicating his reputation. Smith-Dorrien appears to have received no specific responses to the longer private statement, which he sent to Wigram in January 1920 only to find that Fortescue had already sent a copy through an equerry. Nevertheless, if understandably unwilling to be drawn into controversy, the reaction of Wigram to his correspondence during the course of 1919 could only have suggested to Smith-Dorrien that it was his version of events rather than that of French which had triumphed in that particular quarter.[20]

As far as Becke was concerned, Smith-Dorrien's first enquiry as to the accessibility of war diaries relating to Le Cateau preceded the actual War Office authority to prepare a statement by five days. Not actually officially authorised until August 1919, the contact between Becke and Smith-Dorrien then continued until late 1920. Primarily, Smith-Dorrien was seeking the official casualty figures for Le Cateau since he well knew that those given by French were for the whole expeditionary force to that date. It transpired, as he had suspected, that the official figures were 7,812 men and 38 guns. At the same time, Becke was also asked to provide copies of certain orders such as those for II Corps between 21 and 23 August and any details of II Corps' use of roads allocated by such orders to I Corps. Becke was conscientious in compiling 'dossiers' for which Smith-Dorrien was duly grateful and, in return, in December 1919 Smith-Dorrien not only sent a copy of the *Summary of Mis-statements* and two copies of the longer memorandum but in March 1920 also a copy of a statement he had obtained from Haig.[21]

The elicitation of a statement from Haig was one of a series of approaches Smith-Dorrien made to other leading participants in an attempt to refute those allegations in *1914* where contemporary written material was not available. Indeed, Smith-Dorrien had begun to do this as soon as the first extracts were serialised. More often than not, Smith-Dorrien's initial contact was by way of congratulating an individual on some recent honour as a means of extracting some general statement of support for his position[22] but two particular points he needed to clarify were the information available to him on the night of 25/26 August in taking the decision to stand at Le Cateau and what had really transpired during the 'counsel of despair' at Compiegne on 29 August.

Some participants were more willing to assist than others. French's chief of staff in the first campaign, Sir Archibald Murray, had not been attacked in *1914* and, feeling both that Le Cateau should only have been a rearguard action and also that he owed a 'debt of gratitude' to French, Murray would not be drawn into anything other than a most general statement that he had no real recollection of events. Sir William Robertson, who had been Quartermaster General to the Expeditionary Force at the time, believed that French had written a 'really mean & scurrilous book,' but declined to allow Smith-Dorrien to quote wartime conversations, which he claimed should never have taken place between them, or to enter the controversy in any way. Plumer, who had succeeded Smith-Dorrien at Second Army, counselled Smith-Dorrien to remain silent and even Smith-Dorrien's own chief of staff, Forestier-Walker, claimed to have a poor memory. Similarly, the only politician approached, Lord Derby, had no recollection of a conversation, which had taken place between Smith-Dorrien and French in his presence in February 1917, regarding the role in 1914 of Sordet's French Cavalry Corps, whom Smith-Dorrien had always credited with assistance to the Expeditionary Force and French always chosen to ignore.[23]

Haig, whose own attitude towards influencing the judgement of history so closely mirrored that of Smith-Dorrien, had been one of those present at Compiegne. Although claiming not to have actually been there at the same time, Haig was prepared to allow Smith-Dorrien to say of the 'counsel of despair' that 'I can quite honestly say that I have no recollection of your having done such a thing.' Later, Haig responded to the receipt of a copy of Smith-Dorrien's memorandum by sending his own recollections of the retreat, which were those Smith-Dorrien wished him to forward to Edmonds and Becke in early

Introduction                                                                  xvii

1920. Affecting to be 'very lazy on the question of the history of the war' Haig replied that there are 'so many "fairy tales" already in print, especially in French, that if one started taking notice of what has been erroneously written, one's whole life would have to be spent on it.' Generally, too, Haig was relieved by Smith-Dorrien's decision not to make his account public 'as you have many good friends and warm supporters in this country.' In the event, since Haig appeared reluctant to do so, Smith-Dorrien simply sent his own copy of Haig's notes to the Historical Section.[24]

Fortunately, to offset the apparent surfeit of dim recall in the highest echelons of the Expeditionary Force, Smith-Dorrien received substantial assistance from Sir Edmund Allenby, who had commanded the Cavalry Division at that time, and the latter's chief of staff, John Vaughan. It had been Allenby's information in the early hours of 26 August that his cavalry were too worn and scattered to cover any further retreat by II Corps, together with Hubert Hamilton's assessment that 3rd Division was incapable of marching before 9am, that had been the decisive factor in Smith-Dorrien's decision to stand at Le Cateau. Hamilton, of course, was dead although Maurice could fill in some of the detail and Edmonds, who was then serving in the 4th Division, could also vouch for the state of II Corps that morning. However, both Allenby and Vaughan were the best possible witnesses to the information conveyed to Smith-Dorrien at the time and were quite prepared to be quoted. Allenby had also been present at Compiegne and could testify that it was definitely not his recollection that Smith-Dorrien had urged retreat to the coast.[25]

Smith-Dorrien was able to forward his *Summary of Mis-statements* to the War Office on 31 December 1919, commenting in detail on 28 pages of French's book under eight main headings: 'Not an affair of outposts but very heavy fighting' and 'Charges of pusillanimity and pessimism by deprecating the fighting and strength of the enemy, and by comparing the work of the 2nd Corps unfavourably with that of the 1st Corps and Cavalry' with respect to Mons; 'Deprecating the work of the 2nd Corps, by exaggerating the work of the 1st Corps and Cavalry, as well as by confusing the actual work of units of the 2nd Corps' with respect to the retreat from Mons; 'Underestimating the exhaustion of the troops of the 2nd Corps. Incorrect statements as to length of marches and hours of rest, in fact, grave aspersions on the 2nd Corps' and 'By giving an inaccurate account of the conference held by General

Smith-Dorrien and exaggerating the losses at Le Cateau, an attempt made to show that disaster was courted and narrowly escaped' with respect to Le Cateau; 'Successful only by the valour of the troops and the action of British and French Cavalry. No credit due to the Commander is implied' with respect to the continuation of the retreat; 'Exaggeration of the Marne battle in comparison with Mons. Depreciation of the 2nd Corps by appreciation of the work of the 1st and 3rd Corps' with respect to the Marne; and finally, 'Charges of Depression and Pessimism' with respect to the first battle of Ypres.[26]

Smith-Dorrien anticipated that his statement would merely be pigeonholed' but it would always be possible to publish it once he had retired. In the meantime, the longer memorandum running to 60 pages and a further 46 pages of introductory material, which Smith-Dorrien began to distribute to selected recipients on 29 December 1919, could only be beneficial to his interests although he had been careful to have it clearly marked 'Private and Secret. Not to be Made Any Public Use Of,' and to request the eventual return of copies since, as he expressed it to Wigram, he did not wish it to 'fall into the hands of the Enemy.' While elaborating on the same points raised in the statement for the War Office, it went further in advancing an elaborate defence for Smith-Dorrien's refusal to obey French's orders to continue to retreat under Part One, Section 12, Paragraph 13 of *Field Service Regulations*, a point first made by Becke's book. Only 28 copies were circulated and Smith-Dorrien kept a careful record of recipients, most of whom were expected to return the pamphlet when they had read it. As indicated previously, two copies had gone to the Historical Section and a third went to the Assistant Chief of the Imperial General Staff, Sir Charles Harington. Fortescue, Newbolt, Haig, Maurice and Wigram were recipients as were at least 67 others by July 1920. A number were Smith-Dorrien's relatives or junior members of his wartime staff but the list also included the senior field marshals, Lords Methuen and Grenfell; other military figures such as Sir George Barrow, Sir Edward Bulfin, Sir William Lambton, Count Gleichen and Sir William Hickie; and leading journalists such as Leo Maxse and St Loe Strachey. Although not included on the original distribution list, Milner also certainly read the memorandum at the end of 1920.[27]

In addition, there was the copy placed in the British Museum in 1923 at the suggestion of Fortescue. The director, Sir Frederick Kenyon, assured Smith-Dorrien in January 1923 that public access could be

## Introduction

denied for any length of time specified, a similar document by Haig having been 'sealed up for a period of 25 years.' Smith-Dorrien replied in September that he would entrust a copy to the museum once he had finished correcting it in the light of the Official History, merely indicating that it should be secured from access 'until both Lord Ypres and myself have crossed the Styx.' French had been elevated to the earldom of Ypres in 1921.[28]

At this stage in its lengthy preparation - extending eventually to 1948 in the case of the volume concerning the Passchendaele campaign - it was not in the nature of the Official History to make wartime controversies too obvious to the general reader. Thus, the way in which Murray had falsified the timing and dating of orders during the retreat from Mons was carefully concealed by discreet corrections in those reproduced in the volume's appendices. Nor was there any overt reference to French's subsequent interpretation of Smith-Dorrien's role and the text followed the latter's version of events in demonstrating that the decision to stand at Le Cateau had been due to the information brought by Allenby and Hubert Hamilton as to the state of II Corps. There were some minor changes in the second edition published in 1925 after the appearance of the German Official History but nothing which materially altered the official acceptance of the necessity of standing at Le Cateau. In fact, Smith-Dorrien had had a keen sense for the need of an official history at an early stage, suggesting to Wigram as early as January 1915 that an historian - perhaps Leo Amery, who had edited *The Times History of the South African War* and was currently serving on Sir Henry Rawlinson's staff in France - be tasked with collecting contemporary evidence in view of the 'already most inaccurate accounts' being published.[29]

## IV

The publication of the Official History was a significant step in the general acceptance of Smith-Dorrien's version of events in 1914 over that of French. It was available to the public before Smith-Dorrien's retirement from the Gibraltar command, and the army, in September 1923 finally freed him to publish his own personal account. Clearly, it had sufficiently justified Smith-Dorrien for him not to feel the need to be seen to enter into old controversies. He had always claimed that any memoir would be a private one for his sons and then, when he was persuaded to publish, he was initially reluctant to cover the Great War.

As he wrote to Edmonds in August 1924, 'Foolishly or not I am writing memoirs for publication. I had intended to stop short of 1914 but have yielded to pressure, so as to tell the story of the gallant deeds of the II Corps & 4th Division in the Retreat. I make no reference whatever to Lord French's work of fiction *1914* or to his treatment of me.'[30]

Thus, when his book *Memories of Forty Eight Years Service* appeared in April 1925 after serialisation in *The Times* (with thanks to Edmonds and Becke for their assistance - one of Edmond's contributions was to draw maps of Egypt in 1884), only five out of 29 chapters dealt with his wartime command. Smith-Dorrien also indicated that he would have preferred to await the relevant volume of the *Official History* on the circumstances surrounding his resignation. His original memorandum in 1919 had carried the statement that 'I have had too to be specially careful, in defending myself, to avoid sycophancy by giving fulsome praise, and at the same time to say nothing which might injure the reputations of other Generals, especially any of those who served under me.' The memoir was written in much the same vein, Lady Smith-Dorrien also apparently wielding her blue pencil.'[31]

Certainly, the press comment was remarkably uniform, *The Times* referring to 'the dispassionate and clearly expressed statement of the reasons which compelled him to stand and fight at Le Cateau...;' *The Times Literary Supplement* to his correction of others' falsehoods 'temperately and with dignity;' *Country Life* to the 'restraint... to be admired' and *Public Opinion* to his 'fine modesty and restraint.' There were reviews which found the book all too dispassionate, *The Daily Telegraph* referring to 'scant enlightenment,' *Truth* to 'obscurity' and *Punch* to 'stiff references,' which required reading between the lines. Indeed, Smith-Dorrien's account of his escape from Isandhlwana in 1879 received generally more press coverage than the controversies of 1914 but all concluded that he was indeed the man who had saved the expeditionary force, the *Manchester Guardian* even going so far as to remark that Fortescue's assessment of French six years previously had been perfectly justified.[32]

One final addition to the popular association of Smith-Dorrien's reputation with Le Cateau came in the year after the publication of *Forty Eight Years Service*. Smith-Dorrien appeared briefly in *Mons*, one of a series of Great War cinematic 'reconstructions' produced by Harry Bruce Woolfe's company, British Instructional Films, between 1919 and 1927. Variously reviewed as out of focus and overtly sentimental and as

Introduction                                                                xxi

'the most sincere and profoundly moving war picture made in this or any other country,' *Mons* in common with others in the series was made with the co-operation of the War Office and Army Council and utilised serving troops as extras. Generally, only the exploits of Victoria Cross winners were featured but in one scene, as the summary had it, Smith-Dorrien 'watches the marching troops on horseback.'[33]

That no other general was depicted perhaps suggests just how far it was now widely accepted that Smith-Dorrien had been the key figure in the expeditionary force's survival in 1914. French had died in 1925 - Smith-Dorrien had been one of the pallbearers - but, effectively, the judgement of history had been secured in Smith-Dorrien's favour long before.

## Notes

1. *Times Literary Supplement* 26.6.1919

2. Kings College, London: Liddell Hart Centre for Military Archives (hereafter LHCMA), Edmonds Mss, III/16, Unpub. Autobiography, Chap 32, pp. 1-3; Richard Holmes, *The Little Field Marshal* (Cape, London, 1981), pp. 359-360.

3. Sir John Fortescue, *Following the Drum* (Blackwood & Sons, Edinburgh & London, 1931), pp. 286-287; J.F.Naylor, *A Man and an Institution: Sir Maurice Hankey, the Cabinet Secretariat and the Custody of Cabinet Secrecy* (Cambridge University Press, 1984); Peter Fraser, 'Cabinet Secrecy and War Memoirs,' *History* 70, 1985, pp. 397-409.

4. A J Smithers, *The Man Who Disobeyed* (Leo Cooper, London, 1970), p. 132; Tim Travers, *The Killing Ground* (Unwin Hyman, London 1987), pp.15-16 quoting Aylmer Haldane's diary for 23.9.1909. See also LHCMA, Liddell Hart Mss, 11/1933/26 Conversation with Edmonds, 7.12.1933 and PRO, Cab 103/113, Edmonds to Acheson, 30.7.1950.

5. For the state of II Corps when Smith-Dorrien arrived, see Imperial War Museum (hereafter IWM), Smith-Dorrien Mss, 87/47/8, Smith-Dorrien to Murray, 7.5.1919 and *Ibid* to Allenby, 8.5.1919. For examples of Smith-Dorrien's temper, see Congreve Mss, Diary entry for 4.3.1915 and Fortescue, *Following the Drum*, pp. 291-292. On his tenure of the Aldershot Command see R.S.Seim, 'Forging the Rapier among

Scythes: Lieutenant-General Sir Horace Smith-Dorrien and the Aldershot Command, 1907-12.' Unpub. M.A., Houston, 1980.

6. LHCMA, Liddell Hart Mss, 11/1937/4, Liddell Hart conversation with Edmonds, 5.2.1937; Ian Beckett, *Johnnie Gough, V.C.* (Tom Donovan, London, 1989), p.181; PRO, Cab 103/113, Acheson to Edmonds, 27.7.1950.

7. Viscount French, *The Despatches of Lord French* (*The Graphic*, London, 1917), pp. 10-11; R(oyal) A(rchives) Geo V O.1470/23a, Smith-Dorrien journal entries for 4 and 6.9.1914 (Also RA Geo V Q. 823/365 and IWM, 87/47/10); *Ibid*, Q. 832/338, 339, Smith-Dorrien to Wigram, 6 and 9.11.1914.

8. Holmes, *Little Field Marshal*, p.359; IWM, Smith-Dorrien Mss, 87/47/8, General Sir Horace Smith-Dorrien's Statement with regard to the first edition of Lord French's book, '1914'; Field Marshal Lord French, *1914* (Constable, London, 1919), passim.

9. IWM, French Mss, Diary entry 9.5.1919 and French to Bonar Law, 10.5.1919; Richard Holmes, 'Sir John French and Lord Kitchener' in Brian Bond (ed), *The First World War and British Military History* (Oxford University Press, 1991), pp. 113-139.

10. IWM, Smith-Dorrien Mss, 87/47/8, Smith-Dorrien to Milner, 8.5.1919, 14.5.1919, and 5.6.1919; Milner to Smith-Dorrien, 24.5.1919; Smith-Dorrien to War Office, 5.6.1919.

11. IWM, Wilson Mss, HHW 2/1A/19, Wilson to Robertson, 5.6.1919 quoted in Keith Jeffery (ed), *The Military Correspondence of Field Marshal Sir Henry Wilson, 1918-1922* (Bodley Head for the Army Records Society, London, 1985), pp. 104-106; IWM, Smith-Dorrien Mss, 87/47/8, Smith-Dorrien to Milner, 5.6.1919, Brade to Smith-Dorrien, 21.6.1919 and Smith-Dorrien to War Office, 30.6.1919. See the similar statement by Smith-Dorrien to Wigram of 5.6.1919 in RA Geo V O. 1470/6.

12. RA Geo V O. 1470/6 Smith-Dorrien to Wigram, 5.6.1919; *The Times*, 23.6.1919; H.H.Asquith, *The Great Shell Story* (London, 1919); *The Morning Post*, 16.6.1919.

Introduction                                                                                           xxiii

13. Sir John Fortescue, *Author and Curator* (London, 1933), p.249-52; *The Observer*, 29.6.1919; *Quarterly Review* 10.1919, pp. 352-363; Fortescue, *Following the Drum*, pp. 251-298 reproduces the article from *Blackwood's*.

14. RA Geo V O. 1470/23, 25 Fortescue to Wigram of 11.11.1919 and 29.12.1919; IWM, Smith-Dorrien Mss, 87/47/9, 'Register of People to Whom I Show my Statement,' 29.12.1919; Ibid, Kenyon to Smith-Dorrien, 4.1.1923; LHCMA, Maurice Mss, 3/5/101, Fortescue to Maurice, 1/11/1919; Fortescue, *Author and Curator*, p. 253; Keith Grieves, 'Early Historical Responses to the Great War: Fortescue, Conan Doyle and Buchan' in Bond (ed), *First World War and British Military History*, pp.15-40.

15. IWM, Smith-Dorrien Mss, 87/47/8, Newbolt to Smith-Dorrien, 17.2.1919, 5.3.1919 and 10.3.1919.

16. Ian Beckett, 'Frocks and Brasshats' in Bond (ed) *First World War and British Military History*, pp. 89-112; Major-General Sir Frederick Maurice, *Forty Days in 1914* (Constable, London, 1918), p.115.

17. LHCMA, Maurice Mss, 3/5/94-100 Smith-Dorrien to Maurice 1.6.1919, 9.7.1919 and 12.10.1919; IWM, Smith-Dorrien Mss, 87/47/8, Maurice to Smith-Dorrien, 2.9.1919, 4.9.1919, and 6.10.1919. For Maurice's view of Fortescue, see PRO, Cab 45/129 (i), Maurice note, June 1918.

18. IWM, Smith-Dorrien Mss, 87/47/8, Wallace to Smith-Dorrien, 24.6.1919 and 10.7.1919; Major A Corbett-Smith, *The Retreat from Mons* (Cassell, London, 1916), pp.vi-vii, 156, 179, 231-232, 238-253; Holmes, 'Sir John French and Lord Kitchener,' p. 131; A.F.Becke, *The Royal Regiment of Artillery at Le Cateau* (Royal Artillery Institution, Woolwich, 1919), pp. 1,7, 75-76; IWM Smith-Dorrien Mss, 87/47/8, Smith-Dorrien to Allenby, 22.6.1919; Lord Ernest Hamilton, *The First Seven Divisions* (Hurst & Blackett, London, 1916), p.70. See also Army Museums Ogilby Trust, Spenser Wilkinson Mss, OTP 13140, Smith-Dorrien to Wilkinson, 22.8.1919.

19. IWM, Smith-Dorrien Mss, 87/47/8, Smith-Dorrien to War Office, 14.5.1919 and War Office to Smith-Dorrien, 24.5.1919; Ibid, 87/47/10, Copy of journal sent to King; *Ibid*, P.365, Smith-Dorrien Diary entry for 26.9.1914 and 12.9.1914.

20. IWM, French Mss, Diary entry for 9.5.1919: RA Geo V O. 1470/1, Stamfordham to French, 8.5.1919; *Ibid*, 1470/6, Smith-Dorrien to Wigram 5.6.1919; *Ibid* 1470/9, Wigram to Maxwell, 13.6.1919; *Ibid*, 1470/9, Wigram to Maxwell, 13.6.1919; *Ibid*, 1470/10, Wigram to Smith-Dorrien, 13.6.1919; *Ibid*, 1470/27, Wigram to Smith-Dorrien, 21.1.1920.

21. IWM, Smith-Dorrien Mss, 87/47/10, Smith-Dorrien to Becke,16.6.1919, 9.7.1919, 29.7.1919, 7.8.1919, 31.8.1919, 12.10.1919, 11.11.1919, 19.12.1919 and 26.12.1919; Becke to Smith-Dorrien, 28.10.1919, and 13.11.1919; *Ibid*, 87/47/8, Smith-Dorrien to Derby, 15.5.1919; *Ibid*, 87/47/10, Smith-Dorrien to Becke, 7.8.1919, 14.8.1919, 30.9.1919, 21.10.1919, 11.11.1919, 1.12.1919 and 12.12.1919; PRO, Cab 45/129, Smith-Dorrien to Haig, 29.12.1919 and to Becke, 27.3.1920.

22. IWM, Smith-Dorrien Mss, 87/47/8, Replies to Smith-Dorrien from Aylmer Haldane, 15.5.1919; Lawrence, 15.6.1919; Babington 19.6.1919; De Lisle, 26.6.1919; Pole Carew, 30.6.1919; Maxse, 4.7.1919; Grenfell, 16.7.1919, Milne, 22.7.1919; Methuen, 2.8.1919, Altham, 5.8.1919 and Barrow, 9.9.1919.

23. IWM, Smith-Dorrien Mss, 87/47/8, Smith-Dorrien to Murray, 7.5.1919, 26.6.1919, 2.7.1919 and 21.7.1919; Murray to Smith-Dorrien, 18.5.1919 and 12.7.1919; Smith-Dorrien to Robertson, 15.6.1919; Robertson to Smith-Dorrien, 28.5.1919 and 2.7.1919; Plumer to Smith-Dorrien, 11.6.1919; Smith-Dorrien to Forestier-Walker, 13.5.1919 and 26.7.1919; Forestier-Walker to Smith-Dorrien, 23.5.1919. On Sordet, see PRO, Cab 45/129 (iv).

24. IWM, Smith-Dorrien Mss, 87/47/8, Smith-Dorrien to Haig, 8.7.1919; Haig to Smith-Dorrien, 1.7.1919 and 22.7.1919; *Ibid*, 87/47/9, Smith-Dorrien to Haig, 29.12.1919 and 27.3.1920; Haig to Smith-Dorrien, 18.12.1919 and 18.4.1920; *Ibid*, 87/47/10, Smith-Dorrien to Becke, 29.12.1919, 27.3.1920 and 16.4.1920.

25. IWM, Smith-Dorrien Mss, 87/47/8, Edmonds to Smith-Dorrien, nd; Smith-Dorrien to Vaughan, 14.6.1919: Vaughan to Smith-Dorrien, 7.7.1919 and 24.7.1919; Smith-Dorrien to Allenby, 8.5.1919, 30.5.1919 and 29.6.1919: Allenby to Smith-Dorrien, 4.6.1919, 13.7.1919 and 11.10.1919; *Ibid*, 87/47/9, Edmonds to Smith-Dorrien, 18.9.1919.

*Introduction*  xxv

26. IWM, Smith-Dorrien Mss, 87/47/8, Smith-Dorrien to War Office, 31.12.1919; Creedy to Smith-Dorrien, 28.1.1920.

27. RA Geo V O. 1470/25, Fortescue to Equerry, 29.12.1919; *Ibid*, 1470/26 Smith-Dorrien to Wigram, 4.1.1920; *Ibid*, 1470/29 Smith-Dorrien to Wigram, 30.1.1920; Becke, *Royal Artillery*, p.7; IWM, Smith-Dorrien Mss, 87/47/8, Smith-Dorrien Statement; *Ibid*, 87/47/9, Smith-Dorrien to Haig, 29.12.1919; Milner to Smith-Dorrien, 26.12.1920; 'Register of People', 29.12.1919 (with additions to July 1920).

28. IWM, Smith-Dorrien Mss, 87/47/9, Kenyon to Smith-Dorrien, 4.1.1923; Smith-Dorrien to Kenyon, 13.9.1923; David French, 'Sir Douglas Haig's Reputation, 1918-1923: A Note', *Historical Journal* 28, 4, 1985, pp. 953-960. The copy of Smith-Dorrien's memorandum is in British Library Add Mss 52776 whilst a copy of the journal prepared for the King covering the period 21 August to 4 October 1914 is in BL Add Mss 52777.

29. David French, 'Sir James Edmonds and the Official History: France and Belgium' in Bond (ed), *First World War and British Military History*, pp. 69-86 ; *Ibid*, 'Official but not History: Sir James Edmonds and the Official History of the Great War,' *Journal of the Royal United Services Institute for Defence Studies* 131,1, 1986, pp. 58-63 ; Brigadier-General Sir James Edmonds, *Official History of the Great War: Military Operations, France and Belgium, 1914* I, (2nd Ed, Macmillan, London, 1925), pp. 134-137; *Ibid* (3rd Ed, 1933), pp. 140-143; RA Geo V Q. 832/347 Smith-Dorrien to Wigram, 8.1.1915.

30. IWM, Smith-Dorrien Mss, 87/47/9, 'General Sir Horace Smith-Dorrien: The Private Story of his Life for his Sons:' LHCMA, Edmonds Mss, II/I/IIIa, Smith-Dorrien to Edmonds, 12.8.1924. See also RA Geo V 0.1470/6, Smith-Dorrien to Wigram, 5.6.1919.

31. General Sir Horace Smith-Dorrien, *Memories of Forty-Eight Years Service* (John Murray, London, 1925), p.481; Smithers, *Man Who Disobeyed*, p.282.

32. IWM, Smith-Dorrien Mss, 87/47/10a contains a useful series of cuttings from press reviews of the memoirs including *The Times* 2.4.1925; *Times Literary Supplement* 9.4.1925: *Country Life* 2.5.1925; *Public Opinion* 10.4.1925; *Daily Telegraph* 7.4.1925; *Truth* 15.4.1925; *Punch* 8.4.1925; *Manchester Guardian* 3.4.1925.

33. British Film Institute files; Bryher, 'The War from Three Angles', *Close Up*, July 1927, p. 16; *Bioscope*, 23.9.1926, p.33; E.E.B., 'The Man Who Made Mons', *Picturegoer* Jan. 1927, p.31. Originally entitled *The Retreat from Mons*, the film received its first 'trade' showing on 15.9.1926 and was released on 18.11.1926. The British Film Institute archive copy has the reference NFA BS.23.


Quotations from material in the Royal Archives appear by gracious permission of Her Majesty the Queen. Other use of Crown copyright material in the Public Record Office is by permission of Her Majesty's Stationery Office. Grateful acknowledgement is also given to the following for enabling consultation of and quotation from archive material in their possession and/or copyright: the Trustees of the Imperial War Musuem; the Trustees of the Liddell Hart Centre for Military Archives, King's College; the Trustees of the British Library Board and the Library of the British Film Institute; the Army Museums Ogilby Trust. Particular thanks are due to David Smith-Dorrien for allowing reproduction of his father's work.

*To be returned*

*Not fully ~~corrected~~*

## PRIVATE AND SECRET.

The property of General Sir H. Smith-Dorrien, whose statement it is with regard to Lord French's Book "1914."

### CONTENTS.

| | PAGE. |
|---|---|
| Index to Statement. | |
|    Statement ... ... ... ... ... ... | 1 to 60 |
| Appendices. | |
|    A.  Extracts from Diary ... ... ... ... | i. |
|    B.  "Interview" from the Weekly Dispatch ... | x. |
|    C.  Mr. Lovat Fraser's article in do. ... ... | xviii. |
|    D.  Extracts from G. S. Diary of 3rd Division | xxvii. |
|    E.  Memorandum re Resignation of Command of 2nd Army ... ... ... ... | xxix. |
| Map to show certain movements 24th and 25th August. | |

# INDEX.

|  | PAGES. |
|---|---|
| Length of front of 2nd Corps at Mons | 4— 5 |
| Mons, battle of | 6—21 |
| General S.-D.'s request to retire on Bavai | 10 |
| Pessimism of Staff of 2nd Corps | 12 |
| Absence of written orders to retire on 24th August | 16 |
| 1st Corps credited with covering retirement of 2nd Corps | 17—18 |
| Order of the Day thanking General Sordet | 19 |
| Injustice to 15th Brigade | 19—20 |
| Erroneous statement regarding 3rd and 5th Divisions crossing each other | 20 |
| Sir John French's letter to Lord Kitchener praising General S.-D. | 21 |
| True casualties at Mons | 21 |
| Story of the order to retire on Le Cateau | 22 |
| Late start of 1st Corps and failure to reach allotted position at Le Cateau | 22 |
| Quotation from F.S. Regulations | 23 |
| True story of 7th Brigade at Solesmes | 24 |
| True story of movements of Troops night of 25th August | 27 |
| 4th Division not put under the 2nd Corps | 29 |
| True story of why Le Cateau was fought | 30—49 |
| Colonel John Vaughan's letter | 40 |
| Generals D'Amade's and Sordet's help at Le Cateau | 45 |
| Sir J. French's plea of ignorance of General S.-D.'s decision to fight | |
| The "Sauve qui peut" order | 50—53 |
| Accusation of giving a Counsel of Despair | 53 |
| Generals' (Haig, Allenby, Murray) letters | 54 |
| Comparison of Battles of Mons and the Marne | 56 |
| Grave accusation of pessimism | 57 |
| General S.-D.'s appointment to Command an Army | 60 |

## PRIVATE and SECRET.

**Not to be made any public use of except by order of the Army Council.**

# General Sir HORACE SMITH-DORRIEN'S STATEMENT with regard to the first edition of Lord French's Book "1914."

In reply to my request for an official inquiry to enable me to refute the amazing mis-statements regarding myself and the 2nd Corps in Lord French's Book "1914," when it appeared as a serial story in the columns of a daily paper, I was informed that the Army Council could not consent, but they would be glad to receive any statement on the subject I thought fit to make.

Some months have elapsed since then, as it was essential the statement should throughout be supported by the most reliable evidence, and this required time to collect. I have had too to be especially careful, in defending myself, to avoid sycophancy by giving fulsome praise, and at the same time to say nothing which might injure the reputation of other Generals, especially any of those who served under me.

Although a subordinate's actions at times may be faulty, even to the extent of jeopardizing the success of an operation, having dealt with such actions at the time, I regard it as a point of honour to safeguard his reputation and only to make future reference to the incidents if it is in the public interests to do so.

Reference to certain of such incidents which occurred under me in France would undoubtedly bring out points in support of my statement, but I should prefer, rather than drag in the names of the actors, to go to my grave with Lord French's accusations still unrefuted.

I will now commence my statements. My reference to pages are to those in the first edition of "1914." (I hear there is a second edition, but I have not seen it):—

Lord Kitchener's first words to me, when, in response to his order, I entered his room at the War Office on the 18th

August, 1914, expressed grave doubt as to his wisdom in selecting me to succeed the late General Grierson in Command of the 2nd Army Corps; he explained that the Chief of the Staff, General Sir Charles Douglas, had just told him that it would be putting me in an impossible position, as Sir John French had shown great jealousy of, and personal animus towards me for some years, and that such was well known to the Army Council; on my replying that I had no such feelings towards Sir John and that I felt sure I could, by serving him loyally, overcome his dislike, Lord Kitchener adhered to his decision to send me.

For the first six months I certainly succeeded, especially after the battle of Le Cateau, for the Commander-in-Chief was so genuinely grateful to me for having, as he described it, saved his left wing, that he appeared to forget his old animosity, and treated me on the whole with impartiality and gave my Corps praise where praise was due.

He mentioned me in most generous terms in his despatches. In that of 7th September, 1914, he writes of Le Cateau: "**I cannot close this brief account of this glorious stand of the British troops, without putting on record my deep appreciation of the valuable services rendered by General Sir Horace Smith-Dorrien. I say without hesitation that the saving of the left wing of the army under my Command on the morning of the 26th August could never have been accomplished unless a Commander of rare and unusual coolness, intrepidity and determination had been present to personally conduct the operation.**" And later in the same despatch "**It is impossible for me to speak too highly of the skill evinced by the two Generals commanding Army Corps.**" In his despatch of the 8th October, on the Battle of the Aisne, he says :—**I further wish to bring forward the names of the following officers who have rendered valuable services. General Sir Horace Smith-Dorrien and Lieut.-General Sir Douglas Haig I have already mentioned in the present and former despatches for particularly marked and distinguished service in critical situations—since the commencement of the campaign, they have carried out all my orders and instructions with the utmost ability.**"

These *official* despatches HAVE NEVER BEEN OFFICIALLY REPUDIATED.

I would emphasize too that he chose me, with Sir Douglas Haig, to command the two Armies which were formed in January 1915. It was not until the Spring of 1915 that something happened to revive his pre-war animosity towards me. What it was I have not the least idea, but as I have described the position in my memorandum to the Secretary of State for War explaining why, in May 1915, his attitude became so impossible that I resigned Command of the 2nd Army, I will not repeat it here, but attach a copy of that memorandum as an appendix for easy reference.

But even all this cannot account for the virulence of the attack which has been made on me in the book " 1914," and in my own mind I trace the increase in animosity to the account of an interview with me which appeared in the " Weekly Despatch " of February 1917.

I was at that time, with a view to increasing our war efficiency, engaged in an appeal to all managers of public entertainments to which our fighting services were attracted for recreation, to raise their tone, and the Editor of the " Weekly Despatch " was taking a great interest in the matter; he one day asked me on the telephone if I had seen an attack on my handling the troops at Le Cateau in a certain paper, enquiring what the truth was—I replied on the telephone, and the account appeared in the next issue of the " Weekly Despatch."

I am bound to say I knew the Editor intended to use the facts I gave him to reply to the article he was referring to, but, had I understood the account was to appear as from me, I should not have sanctioned its appearance.*

The " INTERVIEW " is printed as Appendix B and also Mr. Lovat Fraser's reply to it the following week, as Appendix C.

Regarding the account of the interview, in so far as the correctness of the statement I made, I have nothing to alter, as these pages will show, and as for Mr. Lovat Fraser's reply I merely put it in to show that he at that time was taking up the cudgels for Lord French, and also because I have referred once or twice to his article in the following pages. I feel sure that had Mr. Lovat Fraser seen these pages, supported by official records, before he wrote his article, he would have drawn deductions less adverse to me—especially in the matter of the hours when the troops of the 2nd Corps reached Le Cateau on 25th. There he appears to have relied largely on an account given by a casual observer who is very materially out, when compared with hard facts from official sources.

I arrived at Landrecies at 3 p.m. on the 21st of August. I knew no more of the situation than the man in the street, having been kept before the war (although holding such important Commands as Aldershot and the Southern) in profound ignorance of all Expeditionary Force plans, latterly

---

*No other statement regarding my services in France has ever been published by me.

not even being allowed to take part in manœuvres,* I motored straight to the Headquarters of my Corps at Bavai, interviewed my new Staff, and hearing Sir John French was at Le Cateau, 25 miles back, went there to obtain his instructions. I was not very cordially received, and this, after what I have said, was to be expected; on page 38 of his book he says that he had asked for Sir Herbert Plumer, and there he showed his acumen, judging from the skill Lord Plumer showed in the endless successes he gained throughout the war.

Realising I should have to be most careful not to give any cause for complaint, I took that opportunity of telling Sir John that H.M. the King had requested me to keep him posted in all pertaining to my Command, but as this involved writing a special diary, I could not do so without his consent, which he readily gave. This diary, parts of which are produced in Appendix A, gives valuable testimony as to my frame of mind. I returned to my Corps, arriving at 11 p.m. Sir John French had given me a certain amount of information about the situation generally, but not much, and the uppermost impression I gained was that my Corps was the left wing of the B.E.F., that the latter, as the left wing of the allied Franco-British forces, was to move next day to the Condé-Mons Canal, prepared for an offensive, and that the canal would merely be a temporary halting place from which we should move forward further into Belgium, pivoting slightly on our right.

The Divisions composing my Corps had not had the advantages of the 1st Corps, in that the Brigades of the latter had in peace time been quartered together at Aldershot, training regularly under the Divisional General, whereas the Brigades forming the Divisions of the 2nd Corps, except occasionally for manœuvres, had only been concentrated after war was declared.

Such, briefly, were the circumstances and conditions under which I took over the Command of the 2nd Corps on the 21st August, '14.

Next day we moved forward to the line of the Canal.

I will now proceed to deal with the chief inaccuracies in Lord French's book so far as I and the 2nd Corps are concerned.

I had been ordered to take up a front of about 21 miles along the Canal, an impossibly long front for a serious action, including as it did the most dangerous salient of the town of Mons itself, and this I pointed out at the Conference on the

---

*Sir John French was then Chief of the Imperial General Staff.

morning of the 23rd August; the C.-in-C. entirely agreed that it would be dangerous to hold on too long to the Mons salient, and that it would be advisable to prepare a position to fall back on across the gorge of the salient, and this Major-General Hubert Hamilton, commanding the 3rd Division, did. Lord French in his book so far from making out my task smaller than it was, says (page 60) that the left of the 5th Division was at Condé itself—now Condé viâ Obourg to Villers St. Ghislain is 23 miles, whilst as a matter of fact* the left of the 5th Division was at Pommeroeuil (5 miles east, and short of Condé) and the right at Givry. I feel sure he did not wish to describe the position inaccurately, but I mention it as illustrating the loose and sketchy manner in which he often records events in the pages of "1914" instead of verifying his facts. For instance, on page 55 he says :—

"The concentration of the British Army had been effected without a hitch."

At this time, viz., on the eve of the Battle of Mons, the 2nd Corps was still without an important part of its Artillery, some of its medical units, and (I think) some of its Field Companies.

P. 55 "The condition of the Reservists was excellent and constantly improving."

As a matter of fact, their condition, *i.e.*, their bodily fitness was anything but good. They were unfit to march, and their discipline left something to be desired. Regimental Officers have said repeatedly that, almost without exception, it was the Reservists of the 5th Division who first broke at Le Cateau.

In view of his implying pusillanimity to me for falling back instead of continuing to fight on the outpost line, it is evident that he considers a twenty-three mile front was a suitable one for two divisions to fight a serious action on.

On page 60 the Field-Marshal says:—"I told the Commanders of the doubts which had arisen in my mind during the previous twenty-four hours, and impressed on them the necessity of being prepared for any kind of move either in advance or in retreat."

I certainly left that Conference firmly impressed with the idea that the Field-Marshal was full of optimism and that we were merely to use the canal position as a jumping off place for a further move into Belgium.

---

*Vide 2nd Corps Operation Order No. 4 of 22 August.

On page 60, giving the situation at 5 a.m. on the 23rd, he says:—"The 2nd Corps had not been seriously engaged whilst the 1st was practically still in reserve." I do not understand this as I am not aware that the 2nd Corps had been engaged at all then. It certainly had had no casualties whereas the 1st Corps must have been engaged on the 22nd for it had 7 casualties that day.

Page 62, "On the morning of the 23rd I left General Smith-Dorrien full of confidence in regard to his position, but when I returned to my Headquarters in the afternoon, reports came to hand that he was giving up the salient of Mons, because the outpost line at Obourg had been penetrated by the enemy, and that he was also preparing to give up the whole of the line of the Canal before nightfall."

War Diaries and official records generally, some of which I have had the opportunity of referring to, prove that it was not merely a penetration of the outpost line, but desperately heavy fighting in which the 3rd Division suffered very heavy losses, the 4th Middlesex on outpost at Obourg losing half their strength fighting brilliantly, whilst the 4th Royal Fusiliers were opposed by 6 times their strength. (3rd Division G.S. Diary*. Appendix D.) These losses and the situation generally decided the G.O.C. of that Division, in view of the C.-in-C.'s expressed anxiety as to the danger of being cut off in the Mons salient, that the time had come to withdraw to the retrenchment S.W. of the town, and I entirely agreed with him.

Regarding my preparation to give up the whole of the line of canal before nightfall, the Field Marshal expressed his astonishment, Page 62, and yet the length of my front, AS HE BELIEVED IT, was twenty-three miles.

I have already explained that it was only about 21 miles, and I would submit that a Commander of two Divisions with his outposts stretched out on a front *even of 21 miles*, along the line of a canal, in full view of, and dominated by hostile positions at point blank range, would be unfit to command if he determined to fight there, rather than fall back (*even as much as three miles*, Page 63) to a more concentrated and defensible position, in view of information that the enemy was in strength, and here I can quote several estimates by Lord French to show that they were in strength.

---

*I have also seen an account by Walter Boem of how the Brandenburg Grenadiers attacked one British Battalion, the 1st Royal West Kents, and in spite of their throwing in a whole Brigade (*i.e.*, 6 Battalions), had to abandon the attack owing to heavy losses, and put outposts.

Page 43. "But nothing came to hand which led us to foresee the crushing superiority of strength which actually confronted us on Sunday, August 23rd."

Writing of the position of the 21st (*i.e., two days before Mons*) he says (pages 46 and 47):—"Exhaustive reconnaissances and intelligence reports admitted of no doubt that the enemy was taking the fullest advantage of his violation of Belgian territory, and that he was protected to the right of his advance at least as far west as Soignies and Nivelles, whence he was moving direct upon the British and 5th French Army." (N.B.—Soignies is only about fifteen miles from Mons).

Describing the shock he received on the morning of the 22nd, on seeing the French Army to the immediate right of him in retreat, and how he at once returned to his Headquarters at Le Cateau, he says (page 57):—"I found there that our own Intelligence had received information which confirmed a good deal of what I had heard in the morning. They thought at least three German Corps were advancing upon us, the most westerly having reached as far as Ath," *i.e.*, 12 miles from our position on the Canal.

Page 58.—Talking of the unreasonableness of General Lanrezac's request brought to him by a Staff Officer at 11 p.m. on the 22nd, he says:—"In view of the most probable situation of the German Army, as it was known to both of us, and the palpable intention of its Commander to effect a great turning movement round my left flank, and having regard to the actual numbers of which I was able to dispose, it is very difficult to realise what was in Lanrezac's mind when he made such a request to me. As the left of the French 5th Army was drawn back as far as Trelon (*N.B.—30 miles south of Mons*) and the centre and right of that Army was in the process of retiring, the forward position I now held on the Condé Canal might quickly become very precarious."

Talking of what was happening at 5 p.m. on the 23rd he says (pages 61 and 62):—"Every report I was now receiving at Headquarters pointed to the early necessity of a retirement of the British Forces," &c., &c.

Sir F. Maurice in his "Forty days in 1914" (page 82), describing the fighting of the 23rd August says, "*two of his (Sir J. French's) divisions, Smith-Dorrien's 3rd and 5th, had in fact been attacked throughout the day by two Corps and two Cavalry Divisions, which had only succeeded in driving back the British from their outpost positions at a cost quite disproportionate to the losses of the defenders, while two more German Corps and the 3rd Cavalry Division had been within reach of the Battlefield but had not taken any real part in the struggle."*

Now the Field Marshal in a paragraph on page 62 says **"Sir Horace need not therefore have feared an imminent turning movement"** though what he means by it, except by way of disparaging me, I do not know. I certainly never said that I feared such a movement, though I submit such a movement might under the circumstances be naturally expected, and ought to be prepared for by any General of experience; this I did.

I further submit that in view of the heavy fighting along my front from 10 a.m., of which, judging from his book, Lord French knows very little, the further statement, (page 62) **" as regards his front, he (Sir Horace) was nowhere threatened by anything more than the Cavalry supported by small bodies of Infantry,"** is a little damaging to the splendid fighting qualities of the 2nd Corps, and is entirely at variance with all the quotations I have given of the Field-Marshal's estimates of the German strength and intentions. Sir F. Maurice in his "Forty days in 1914" (page 78) says of the 23rd of August, *"The battle opened in earnest about 10.30 a.m. with a bombardment of some batteries of the 3rd Corps which came into action to the north of Obourg, and from that time onwards the line of guns was gradually extended westward as battery after battery, first from the 3rd Corps and then from the 4th Corps, came into action, until by 1 p.m. the Germans had established a great superiority in artillery along the front of Sir Horace Smith-Dorrien's Corps. Under the cover of this bombardment the Infantry of the 3rd Corps began soon after 11 a.m. an attack in mass on the loop of the Canal north of Mons."*

(Page 81 of Maurice).—*"Further west along the Canal the attacks of the extreme right of the 3rd Corps and of the 4th Corps, which had rather further to go to reach the battlefield, developed somewhat later than the attack on Mons itself, and were if anything less successful, despite the great superiority of German artillery; less than half the Infantry of Sir C. Ferguson's 5th Division met these attacks, and was able to hold the general line of the Canal until dusk, when it, like the 3rd Division, was withdrawn to an entrenched position in rear."*

I have quoted from Lord French's book all the statements which bear on the subject of the extent of the German threats and all are pretty convincing of their seriousness, and in the face of them I ask what would have been said of me, had I reinforced my outpost line to such an extent as to be unable to fall back to a more concentrated, previously selected, and entrenched position. But in fairness to the Field-Marshal I must point out that the book was written four years after the event, and it is possible that he regards the estimate he gave *in his official despatch, dated 7th September, 1914*, as the correct one, for there he gives no indication of the serious situation he describes in his book. He says nothing there about his seeing the French retiring on his right on the morning of the 22nd, or of the news brought to him, at 11.30 p.m. on that day that the 5th French Army had retired, and that its left, which ought to have been in touch with his right was already at Trelon, 28 miles south of Mons (which indicates a gap of 18 miles, the right of the B.E.F. being at Grand Renz), or of the strength of mind he must have exercised to have remained to fight on the 23rd far from any support, with both his flanks *en l'air* especially in the face of his instructions from Lord Kitchener as Secretary of State which Lord French gives on page 14 as follows:—

"*Therefore while every effort must be made to coincide most sympathetically with the plans and wishes of our Ally the gravest consideration will devolve upon you as to participation in forward movements where large bodies of French troops are not engaged, and where your force may be unduly exposed to attack. Should a contingency of this sort be contemplated, I look to you to inform me fully and give me time to communicate to you any decision to which H.M.'s Government may come to in the matter.*"

He merely says (vide despatch) "**at 6 a.m. on August 23rd I assembled the Commanders of the 1st and 2nd Corps and Cavalry Division—and explained the general situation, &c. —from information I received from French Headquarters I understood that little more than one or at most two of the enemy's Army Corps with perhaps one Cavalry Division were in front of my position, and I was aware of no attempted outflanking movement.**"

The impression I got from the Conference at my Headquarters at 6 a.m. on the 23rd was that Sir John was full of optimism. He certainly gave no hint (that I heard) of the French having retired on our right, and had he done so, I am inclined to think it might have been beyond my powers to have shown the optimism he credits me with when he left me on the morning of the 23rd (page 62).

As it was though, I was full of optimism and I never lost that optimism, but, as the Germans advanced and I was able to appreciate that their numbers were large, I took up a fighting position, and, thanks to the grand qualities of my troops, was quite content with the result of our action on the 23rd, and ready to carry on the battle on the 24th.

On page 62, the Field Marshal talking of what was happening on the afternoon of the 23rd says : **He (General S. D.) said that he anticipated a gap occurring in his line between the 3rd and 5th Division, in the neighbourhood of** *Mariette* **and he went so far as to make a request for help to the 1st Corps"** and later on "**The General's anxiety seems to have been lessened later in the afternoon, for at 5 p.m.,** etc."

Therefore he states that before 5 p.m. I applied to the 1st Corps for help.

The true story is that the 3rd Division, after desperate fighting, retired to a position in the neighbourhood of Frameries, but the Germans, who had crossed the Canal further west, had, about 7 p.m., got into Frameries, 3½ miles S.W. of *Mariette*, and were between the 3rd and 5th Divisions, with nothing to stop them. The G.O.C. 3rd Division realising the seriousness of the situation appealed to me. I had no reserve to give him, but I knew General Haking's 5th Brigade of the 1st Corps was 5 kilometres from the spot, where the enemy were said to be breaking through, and as there was no time to lose, I jumped into a motor and got to Sir D. Haig's Headquarters in a quarter of an hour. I found there Major F. Maurice (now Major-General Sir F. Maurice retired) on the same mission direct from General Hubert Hamilton. Sir Douglas first offered mounted troops, but as it was getting dark, I urged that, by the time they got there, Cavalry could not act, and he accordingly consented to send Infantry. Major Maurice took the order to General Haking who just arrived in time to save the break through.

On page 63 the Field Marshal says : "**At 7·15 a.m. he (General S. D.) asked for permission to retire on Bavai.**" This is only a half truth, and it is a pity that he did not quote the whole of my message, though had he done so he would not have furthered what appears to be a main object of his book, namely, to discredit me. The full message was as follows :—
"*To G.H.Q. G. 271, August 23rd, 3rd Division reports at 6·47 p.m. the Germans are in front of his main position and are not attacking at present, they are, however, working round 3rd Division on left flank. If it should appear that there is a danger of my centre being pierced, I can see no course but to order a general retirement on Bavai position. Have I your permission to adopt this course, if it appears to be necessary?*

*From 2nd Corps, 7·15 p.m. (Signed) Oxley, Colonel.*

A General's duty is to look ahead and prepare for eventualities. The break through by the enemy did not take place, thanks to General Haking's 5th Brigade, as already described. It must be remembered that although I had already greatly contracted my front, it was still far too large for the troops I had, and every man was in the front line so that a break through, with no reserves to meet it, must have entailed retreat.

N.B.—On the morning of the 24th the front of the 2nd Corps was about 12 miles in length or about double that of the 1st Corps. By way of comparison I would mention that at Le Cateau, where I was able to choose a position suitable for fighting a delaying action, the extreme front was only 9 miles, and there I had 10 Brigades available, whereas in my front of 12 miles on the 23rd and 24th I had only 6 Brigades.

Neither Sir John French's Chief of the Staff, Sir Archibald Murray, or my own Chief Staff Officer, Brigadier General F. Walker, recognise the Field Marshal's statement, and one can hardly be surprised.

The former writes:—"*Regarding the statement "at 7·15 p.m. 23rd of August he (S. D.) asked for permission to retire on Bavai," I am unable to support this statement and cannot credit that it was made,*" and the latter:—"*As regards the statement made by Lord French on page 63 of "1914" that at 7·15 p.m. on the 23rd August, 1914, the G.O.C. 2nd Corps asked for permission to retire on Bavai, I have no recollection of any such message having been sent, nor was the necessity of doing so even mentioned to me by Sir Horace Smith-Dorrien or by me to him. On the contrary we fully expected to be ordered to hold our ground on the morrow and I have every reason to believe that the Corps Commander was as confident as I was, that, as far as can be foreseen in war, we should be able to do so. The only grounds for anxiety lay, first, in the lodgment which the enemy had made on the left of the 3rd Division, (from which he was subsequently ejected by troops lent by the 1st Corps) and secondly, in the possibility that the enemy might succeed in enveloping the left flank of the Cavalry Division which was guarding the left of the 2nd Corps, some indications of a far-reaching envelopment having become apparent during the day. Naturally, Staff arrangements for a retirement in case it should be enforced were made, but I am positive that the necessity for retirement or the probability of having to retire were never mentioned to me by the Corps Commander.*"

I call attention to the entry for this day the 23rd August in my diary (App. A) and submit that the optimistic style it is written in hardly bears out the tone of Lord French's criticisms. A wish to retire never entered my head and I am sure that all my staff will repudiate any imputation of pessimism or pusillanimity at any time they served with me. I have already said that the impression I got from Sir John at the

Conference on the 23rd was that we were to advance from the Canal, and my Chief Staff Officer will bear witness to my surprise when, at about 3·30 a.m. on the 24th, he returned from G.H.Q. (where he had gone by the C.-in-C.'s order) saying we were to retire, and I was to arrange a plan with Sir Douglas Haig.

It is evident too that the Field-Marshal clung to the idea of the offensive to the last, and may unwittingly have given me the impression that retreat was most unlikely, for (on page 63) on getting the news on the evening of the 23rd of the French misfortunes he says :—" **Appreciating the situation from the point of view which all reports now clearly establish, my last hope of an offensive had to be abandoned.**"

Sir John French in his despatch of 7th September, '14, says he got the news which made the retirement a necessity *at 5 p.m. on the 23rd.* In his book, page 63, Lord French fixes *11·30 p.m. on the 23rd as the hour,* but adds " **it clearly showed that our position was strategically untenable, but this conclusion had been forced upon me** *much earlier in the evening,* **when I received a full appreciation of the situation as it then appeared at French Head Quarters. General Joffre also told me that his information led him to expect that I might be attacked next day by at least 3 German Corps and 2 Cavalry Divisions.**"

Why Sir John did not take me into his confidence or take some action *earlier in the evening,* I cannot say. If I had been able to withdraw impedimenta and form my troops for retirement under cover of night, the desperate fighting of the 5th Division on the 24th would have been avoided.

Page 64.—The Field-Marshal, talking of the line he had selected to retire on, *i.e.,* Jerlain-Maubeuge, says " **The Corps and Divisional Staff Officers who were called into Headquarters to receive orders,** *especially those of the 2nd Corps,* **thought our position was much more seriously threatened, and, in fact, one or two expressed doubts as to the possibility of effecting retirement in the presence of the enemy in our immediate front.**"

Regarding his emphasising the pessimism of the Staff Officers of the 2nd Corps, I must explain that only one Staff Officer attended from that Corps, namely, Brigadier General Forestier-Walker, and he was ordered in by name (O. (*a*) 92 23 Augt. G.H.Q. 8·17 p.m.). The 2nd Corps was the only one in close grip with the enemy, and it would have been surprising if its Chief Staff Officer had not realised the gravity of the task; the following statement by him is illuminating on several points:—

"3. *With reference to the assembly of Staff Officers at G.H.Q. on the night of the 23rd August ("1914" page 64):*

    (a) *I was the only representative present of the 2nd Corps, and I arrived at G.H.Q., which was then at Le Cateau, at about 11 p.m. on the night of the 23rd, as well as I can remember.*

    (b) *Neither to the C.-in-C. nor to the C.G.S. did I ever express doubt as to the possibility of effecting a retirement in the presence of the enemy in our immediate front.*

    (c) *I informed the C.G.S. that the hostile lodgment, alluded to, must give ground to some little anxiety, but that a counter-attack by two Battalions, which the 1st Corps had been asked to lend for the purpose, should clear the position.*[*]

    *I informed Sir Archibald Murray that Sir Horace considered that, so far, there was no reason to apprehend that the 2nd Corps would be unable to hold its own front on the morrow, and that he would be prepared to take his part in an offensive if such were decided upon, but that an offensive would have to be undertaken by troops holding the front line, together with their local reserves.*

    (d) *Sir A. Murray then left the room to take the C.-in-C.'s orders, and returned, after an interval, with the C.-in-C.'s orders for a general retirement, which he communicated verbally to the assembled Staff Officers. So far as the 2nd Corps was concerned, these orders were to the following effect:*

        *The 2nd Corps was to retire to the neighbourhood of Bavai in concert with the 1st Corps on its right. The retirement was to commence at 5 a.m., and, as regards the two Corps, co-ordination was to be arranged by the Corps Commanders in consultation.*

        *No written orders for the retirement were issued at the time, or received before the retirement had commenced.*

---

[*]This had actually been effected at the time, but news of it had not come in when I left the Corps to go to G.H.Q.

*No orders were given to the 2nd Corps that "the 1st Army Corps was to move up towards Givry and to take up a good line to cover the retreat of the 2nd Corps towards Bavai," as implied on page 64 of "1914."*

*On the contrary, I urged strongly that, in view of the short time available to the two Corps Commanders to arrange a meeting, consult, and issue orders, G.H.Q. should themselves decide at once which of the two Corps should move first, or whether the move should begin simultaneously. It was, however, decided to adhere to the instructions already given, viz., that the matter was to be decided between the two Corps Commanders. If any instructions modifying the above were given by G.H.Q., they never reached 2nd Corps before the movement had commenced, and I never heard of them.*

(e) *Sir John French sent for me before my departure from G.H.Q. and after talking about the sad death of Sir J. Grierson, questioned me shortly about the situation. I told him that the Corps Commander was quite confident of his ability to hold his own front on the 24th, provided that his left flank was secure. The C.-in-C. then told me that he had given orders for the retirement on account of the movements of the French.*

(f) *I left G.H.Q. at about 1 a.m., 24th August, and arrived back at 2nd Corps H.Q. at between 3 and 3·30 a.m.*

*I read to the Corps Commander the notes which I had taken, and which embodied the instructions which I have already quoted.*

*Before leaving G.H.Q., I had asked the B.G.G.S. 1st Corps to try to arrange the earliest possible meeting between Sir Douglas Haig and Sir Horace at 2nd Corps H.Q., and Sir Douglas arrived there at, I think, about 4·30 a.m."*

G. Forestier-Walker,
Major-General.

Wilton,
3/8/19.

As these Staff Officers only reached G.H.Q. about 11 p.m. on the 23th-24th, and left two to two and a half hours later, the C.-in-C. should have realised that they could not get back to their own headquarters and explain the situation to their respective G.O.C.s in time for orders to retire reaching the troops before daylight.

When my B.G.G.S. (Brigadier General Forestier-Walker) returned to me at 3 or 3·30 a.m. and told me that I was to arrange a retirement with Sir Douglas Haig, I at once wrote a personal note to the Field Marshal, telling him that it would be well after daylight before any orders could be carried out by the troops, and that, before a retirement could commence, my impedimenta (closed up for a battle) must be got away and the roads be cleared. I concluded by saying "*I have told you this so that you may realise the situation and that the operation we are embarking on is one of the most difficult which can occur, namely, breaking off a fight at its hottest and adopting retirement tactics, without offering great advantages to an enemy.*" This personal letter was acknowledged thus:—"**To Sir Horace Smith-Dorrien, O (a) 203, 24th August. Just received your private communication, hope to see you at Sars La Bruyère after visiting Haig. I leave Bavai at 7 a.m.—From French.**" The wire is timed out at 7·15 a.m.

Had the Field Marshal, when he had definitely made up his mind to retire, whether at 5 p.m. according to his official despatches, or 11·30 p.m. on the 25th according to his book, sent written retirement orders to the Headquarters of the Corps Commanders, most valuable time would have been saved, whereas by sending for senior General Staff Officers to go in to G.H.Q. (the return journey being between 50 to 70 miles), to obtain verbal instructions for their Generals to arrange among themselves a plan of retreat, he precluded all hope of their having the advantages of night to slip away in. It is unnecessary to draw attention to the disadvantage a General is placed at, by having his directing Staff Officer taken away for 6 or 7 hours in the middle of a serious operation.

The curious thing is that the order calling in Staff Officers into G.H.Q. to receive orders for a retreat was timed G.H.Q. 8·17 p.m. and yet the following order timed 8·40 p.m. was sent from the C.-in-C. to 1st and 2nd Corps and Cavalry Division: "**O (a) 95, August 23rd. It seems probable that the enemy may develop his attack to-night or to-morrow. I will stand this attack on the ground now occupied by the troops. You will therefore strengthen your position by every possible means. Report to Feignies, 3 miles N.W. of Maubeuge from 7 a.m. to-morrow—acknowledge**" so it is evident that there was indecision or confusion somewhere.

Lord French (page 64) says: "**However, I determined to effect a retreat and orders were issued accordingly—the 1st Army Corps was to move up towards Givry and to take up a good line to cover the retreat of the 2nd Corps towards Bavai, which was to commence at daybreak.**"

I have no more knowledge of such orders than Major-General Sir G. Forestier-Walker. *No written orders at all were given*, in fact it appears from the G.H.Q. August operation order file that no written order was issued between the one at 11˙35 p.m. 21st August ordering the Cavalry to the western flank of the B.E.F., and the one issued at 8˙25 p.m. on 24th August ordering the retirement of the B.E.F. to the Le Cateau position. There is, however, strong evidence that the C.-in-C. gave no distinct plan of action, for in the G.S. diary of the 1st Corps appear two messages from Br. General J. Gough, V.C. (who was the S.G.S.O. of the 1st Corps ordered in to G.H.Q. at Le Cateau by the C.-in-C.), sent off by him from the G.H.Q. to the 1st Corps.

"*To 1st Corps, G (a) 6. 24th August. Orders to fall back owing I gather to news from French. Our line is to be La Longueville to La Boiserette, 4 miles west of Bavai, all impedimenta should move at once to south of Meuse about Pont Sur Sambre, the retirement to take place early, but have not yet received detailed instructions.*"

From Gough (S.G.S.O. 1st Corps), Le Cateau,
1 a.m., received 1˙27 a.m.

"*To 1st Army, G (a) 7, August 24. Continuation of my G (a) 6. C.-in-C. orders that the 2nd Corps retires under cover of 1st Corps, Cavalry to make demonstration. Corps Commanders to arrange cooperation in retirement: suggest meeting between Sir D. Haig and General Smith-Dorrien. Roads through Fortress of Maubeuge not available. Malcolm and I have discussed operation. He knows my views. Suggest the left of corps be looked after particularly and line Bonnet to Blaregnies be firmly established before our left is withdrawn. Coming back in motor.*"

From Gough (S.G.S.O. 1st Corps), LE CATEAU,
1˙30 A.M., received 1˙55 a.m.

It will be of interest here to read the entries in my diary for these days. (Appendix A.)

After Br. General Forestier-Walker's return to my H.Q. at Sars-la-Bruyère much had to be done before definite orders could be issued, though of course a brief warning order was issued at once. In the first place my consultation with Sir D. Haig had to take place, and orders based on it had to be framed and sent to Divisions and thence to the smaller units. The 2nd Corps had to remain holding its position to cover the 1st Corps falling back and it was 6˙30 a.m. before the 3rd Division (the first of the 2nd Corps to retire) sent out orders to its first Brigade, the 8th, to fall back (3rd Division G.S. Diary, G. 172 of 24th August).

In any case, judging from the time, 1 a.m. or later*, when the Staff Officers left G.H.Q. with their long drive through strange roads encumbered with fugitives on foot and in carts, it should have been evident to the Supreme Command that it was impossible for the 2nd Corps to commence retiring by daylight. My Staff Officer, Br. General Forestier-Walker, only reached my Headquarters about 3 to 3·30 a.m. when daylight was almost breaking, the sun rising about 5 a.m.

Page 65. The Field Marshal claims that at 5·30 a.m., when he went out to his advanced headquarters at Bavai, he found **" that the orders issued through the night had been carried out and that the 1st Corps was then on the line Nouvelles-Harmignies-Givry, with Headquarters at Bonnet,"** and if this was really the case, some strength is lent to the statement made in Maurice ("40 days in 1914," page 89) as follows:—
*" Sir D. Haig on the British right had had information on the previous evening of the retreat of the 5th French Army, and before the receipt of Sir John French's orders, had made all preparation for the withdrawal which he saw to be inevitable—on the receipt of these orders he was able to slip away early in the morning before Von Kluck's 9th Corps had completed its preparations."*

There is confirmatory evidence of the 1st Corps having knowledge of the intended retirement on the 23rd, for in the 1st Division order file, there is 1st Division Order No. 4, *dated 23rd August, 1914,* commencing "*the left wing of the army is ordered to march back and uncover the north face of Maubeuge, the division will move in 3 groups.*" Then follows the detail of each group, roads, trains, etc., and written in pencil on the order, " N.B.—Not issued, but acted on in a modified form."

I incline to the view that it was Sir Douglas Haig's own foresight which had enabled him to appreciate on the 23rd that a retirement would be probable, for he was in touch with the general situation, which I, as I have already explained, was not.

Lord French makes a statement on page 65 " **they (the 1st Corps) were making an excellent stand to cover the retirement of the 2nd Corps.**"

In the first instance the 2nd Corps were making the stand, whilst the 1st Corps retired.

---

*The B.G.G.S. 1st Corps was evidently still at G.H.Q. at 1·30 a.m. for that is the hour on a message he sent to his Corps.

As a specimen of sketchy writing, on pages 65 and 66 Lord French describes how from the H.Q. of the 1st Corps at Bonnet, he had watched the fighting of the Cavalry Division and 19th Brigade under Allenby, to the west flank of the 5th Division. Now from Bonnet to Andregnies, where the fighting was, is 11 or 12 miles as the crow flies, so it is obvious that he cannot have framed the sentence very carefully.

On page 66. He mentions the troops in this part of the line (namely, the 1st Corps) as being **"very active and pushing"** and proceeds to mention in detail the Battalions of the 8th Brigade under Davies amongst these troops, as part of the 2nd Division, *i.e.*, of the 1st Corps.

Inadvertently he has given praise to troops under myself, for the 8th Brigade commanded by "Doran" (not by Davies as stated by the Field Marshal) was part of the 3rd Division of the 2nd Corps. That Brigade on the right of the 3rd Division fought brilliantly on the 23rd and 24th, and I am glad that, by being mistaken for part of the 1st Corps, it has received praise which it so thoroughly earned.

Pages 65 and 66. Great praise is given to the 1st Corps for standing to cover the retirement of the 2nd Corps, the description indicating determined fighting, and Sir John concludes by saying—**"the steadfast attitude and skilful retreat of our right wing at Mons had much to do with the success of our withdrawal, and the short time I spent with the 1st Corps inspired me with great confidence.**

It is I think interesting to note that their total casualties on this day were only 45, whilst ours were 2,926.* The 2nd Corps too had lost 1,482* officers and men on the previous day as compared with 29 in the 1st Corps.

I do not wish in any way to detract from the credit given to the 1st Corps, and no one could question its skilful leading and proved fighting efficiency, but I am bound to defend my own Corps, concerning which in his official despatch of 7th September '14, he says himself: **"The 2nd Corps retired on and entrenched the line Dour Querouble-Frameries and enabled the 1st Corps to withdraw and reach the line Bavai-Maubeuge at about 7 p.m."**

It is impossible to understand why, after 5 years, he should reverse his verdict given when events were fresh in his mind; then he gave the 2nd Corps credit for enabling the 1st Corps to retire—now the boot is on the other leg. As a matter of fact the two Corps mutually helped each other to retire, as agreed on by Sir D. Haig and myself at our meeting on the

---

*These figures do not include Staff Divisional Cavalry, Artillery or anything except Infantry.

morning of the 24th—we having to make our own arrangements in the absence of any written plan from the C.-in-C.

On page 68 he describes a visit he paid to General Sordet, and concludes by saying: "**He promised however to do all in his power to help me, and as my story will presently show he kept his word splendidly.**"

I subscribe to these last 5 words, and the following copy of an order of the day, published by me on the 29th August, will show that I took the earliest opportunity of publicly expressing my appreciation of General Sordet's help:—

*ORDER OF THE DAY.*

*Headquarters,*

*2nd Army Corps,*

*29th August, 1914.*

*As it is improbable the troops of the 2nd Army Corps understand the operations of the last few days, commencing on the 21st instant with the advance to the line of the MONS Canal and ending with a retirement to our present position on the River OISE about NOYON, the Commander of the Corps desires to let Troops know that the object was to delay the advance of a far superior force of the enemy to enable our Allies to conduct operations elsewhere. This object, owing to the skilful handling of the Commanders of units and the magnificent fighting spirit shown by all ranks against overwhelming odds, and in spite of very heavy casualties, was achieved, and the French Army is now reported to be advancing.*

*That the losses were not greater in the retirement from the HANCOURT-CAUDRY-BEAUMONT-LE CATEAU position on the 26th inst. is due largely to the support given by French troops, chiefly General Sordet's Cavalry Corps, operating on the West flank of the British Troops, and we may well be thankful to our gallant comrades in arms.*

*General Sir Horace Smith-Dorrien, whilst regretting the terribly heavy casualties and the weary forced marches, in which it has been impossible to distribute the necessary amount of food, begs to thank all ranks and to express his admiration of the grand fighting and determined spirit shown by all ranks, and his pride in being allowed to command such a splendid force.*

*He is sure that whenever it is thought necessary to again assume the offensive, the Troops will be as pleased as he will himself.*

On page 70 Lord French says: "**The action of the Cavalry and 19th Bde. had greatly relieved the heavy pressure on the 5th Division.**"

Surely some credit is due to that Division's own flank guard. This was the gallant 15th Bde. which fought with wonderful tenacity, losing over 1,100, one-third of its fighting strength, whereas the 19th Bde. only lost 40 that day.

On page 71 he says: "**There was some confusion in the retirement of the 2nd Corps, the 5th Division crossed the rear of the 3rd near Bavai, got to the east of them and somewhat on the line of the retreat of the 1st Corps whose movement was thus hampered and delayed.**"

In the first place the statement is incorrect, for it was the 3rd Division which crossed the rear of the 5th, and in the second place, even were it true, the accusation of confusion and hampering the 1st Corps is most ungenerous. What happened was this:—In order to fall back clear of Maubeuge, it was impossible for the British Army to retire straight to the rear, and the whole retirement was diagonal to the left rear (or S.W. instead of due south). The town of Bavai was indicated as the point of junction between the two Corps.

Owing to the heavy fighting in which the 5th Division was engaged, and the pressure by the enemy on its west or outer flank (*on which the Field Marshal lays stress in page 71*) it was impossible for the 2nd Corps to move further to the West, or for the 5th Division to retire as quickly as the 3rd Division.

Consequently the latter* was moved across the rear of the 5th Division on to the Jerlain-Bavai road, partly to make room for the 1st Corps, and partly to take up a covering position against the outflanking German movement, so as to allow the heavily pressed and weary 5th Division to fall back into a protected area on the right of the 3rd Division and between it and Bavai.

I submit a by no means unskilful rearguard move. If in its retirement it hampered the 1st Corps I much regret it, but I had not heard of this until I read Lord French's book 5 years after the event. My B.G.G.S. writes regarding that occasion that he has some recollection of the two Corps impeding each other's movements, but is under the impression that it was due to the 1st Corps using a road allotted to the 2nd; of this however I have no confirmation.

* The 7th Infantry Brigade of 3rd Division has this entry in its diary:— "Reached Bavai about 4 p.m. After a short halt in a field we received orders to move at once towards Wargnies to support 5th Division if necessary. The Brigade halted at Le Plat de Bois, pushing out outposts to the north." (N.B.—Wargnies is 6½ miles due west of Bavai.)

A glance at the map* showing the position of the two Corps on the morning of the 24th August, and the direction of the roads, converging as they do on Bavai, will make it apparent to anyone that they were likely to impede each other's movements in Bavai. On the morning of the 24th the British Army was on a front of 24 miles and during that day's fighting it had to retire and contract to a front of 12 miles. It was, to say the least of it, unnecessary of the Field Marshal to make capital of the incident even to injure the reputation of the 2nd Corps, and further it was hardly wise without being sure of his facts.

As this brings us to the evening of the 24th, it seems a suitable place to quote from a letter, written on the 25th August, from the C.-in-C. British Expeditionary Force, Sir J. French, to the S. of S., Lord Kitchener: "**I cannot speak too highly in praise of all ranks, but in particular I must mention the two Army Corps Commanders, Smith-Dorrien and Haig, and Allenby, they directed their Commands with the utmost skill.**" Comment is unnecessary, but it would not be unfair to suggest that the Field Marshal regards this letter, written when events were fresh in his mind, in the same category as his September 1914 official despatch.

Page 7: "Our losses in the fighting of the last TWO DAYS were considerable, but not excessive, having regard to the nature of the operation." It is interesting to record what these casualties actually were :—

    1st Corps ... ... ... ... ... Total    74
    2nd Corps ... ... ... ... Total 3,819†
    Cavalry ... ... ... ... ... Total  257

Page 72: "**In the early hours of the 25th the retreat was continued.**" I think it right here to recount what happened regarding orders for the retreat.

At 6 p.m. on the 24th I reported myself to the C.-in-C. at his advanced headquarters at Bavai, described the situation in the 2nd Corps, and asked for instructions as to further movements.

He replied that I could do as I liked, and that Sir D. Haig was going to start at 5 a.m. I remonstrated, saying that unless we moved early it would be a case of that day over again, when orders had been issued too late to avoid the

---

*The map to save confusion shows billeting areas of 3rd and 5th Divisions separate whereas there was some overlapping.

†These figures include nothing but Infantry and omit the casualties in 2/ Suffolks, their losses being included in those given at Le Cateau on 26th August. The total for the Corps therefore was well over 4,000, *i.e.*, about 17% of its Infantry war strength.

enemy coming to close grips. He asked me what I proposed. I replied that I wished to start off my impedimenta (which would have rested many hours), soon after midnight, followed by troops at such times as would ensure my rearguard being clear of the Jerlain-Bavai road by 5 a.m. Sir J. French concurred, remarking that Sir D. Haig could still do as he intended.

Sir A. Murray, the Chief of Staff, was working at a table in the room, and I went across to him and told him it was essential we should move as an army, and implored him to get the Chief to issue an Army Order saying that the whole Force would move as I had suggested.

I have already described how it had been left to Sir D. Haig and myself to plan our retirement on the morning of the 24th, and I have recited this incident as illustrating the evident dislike at that time of the C.-in-C. to issue definite *written* orders. That night an Army Order, timed 8˙25 p.m., duly appeared ordering the Force to move to the Le Cateau position, being clear of the Jerlain-Bavai-Maubeuge, by 5˙30 a.m.

It is interesting to read, in connection with the above, Lord French's statement on page 71 in describing events of the 24th August: "**I therefore abandoned all such ideas and issued orders** *at about 3 p.m.* **directing the retreat some miles further back to the line Le Cateau-Cambrai.**" There is no record of this order, and had it been received by me I should not have gone to the Field-Marshal at 6 p.m. to enquire what were his instructions for my Corps.

Apparently something went wrong, and on page 74 the Field Marshal actually says so, "**The 1st Corps was delayed in starting for several hours and was only able to reach the neighbourhood of Landrecies, so that at the conclusion of the day's march a somewhat dangerous gap** (N.B.—8 miles, vide Field Marshal's book, page 81) **existed between the 1st and 2nd Corps.**"

It would have been interesting if he had told us in his book why the gap occurred, and I cannot help feeling that had my Corps been the one to fail in carrying out his orders, the matter would not have been passed over in silence.

Had there been no gap, in other words, had the 1st Corps been in line with the 2nd Corps on the Le Cateau position on the night of the 25th, and had the C.-in-C. remained near enough to the front to handle the two Corps, a much more favourable state of affairs should have resulted.

I note that on page 75 he particularly gives credit to the 1st Corps for "**still proceeding, although the troops were very tired and handicapped also by heavy rearguard fight-**

ing, to carry out instructions in excellent order and with complete efficiency."

N.B.—The total casualties in the 1st Corps on the 25th, chiefly in the attacks on their bivouacks after dark at Landrecies and Maroilles, were 196. This remark is evidently put in to give an impression of shortcomings on the part of the 2nd Corps, *which had carried out the orders to the letter in spite of heavier fighting, longer marches (vide map) and far heavier losses.*

On the 26th instant, however, I fully admit that I disobeyed orders, but under circumstances which an impartial C.-in-C. would I am sure have considered justifiable, and which are provided for by regulations as follows:—

FIELD SERVICE REGULATIONS PART I.
SECTION 12, PARAGRAPH 13.

13. Notwithstanding the greatest care and skill in framing orders, unexpected local circumstances may render the precise execution of the orders given to a subordinate unsuitable or impracticable. Under such circumstances the following principle should guide an officer in deciding on the course of action:—

    i. A formal order should never be departed from either in letter or print—(a) so long as the officer who issued it is present; (b) if the officer who issued the order is not present, providing there is time to report to him and await a reply without losing an opportunity or endangering the Command.

    ii. A departure from either the spirit or the letter of an order is justified if the subordinate who assumes the responsibility bases his decision on some fact which could not be known to the officer who issued the order, and if he is conscientiously satisfied that he is acting as his superior, if present, would order him to act.

    iii. *If a subordinate in the absence of a superior neglects to depart from the letter of his order when such departure is clearly demanded by circumstances and failure ensues, he will be held responsible for such failure.*

    iv. Should a subordinate find it necessary to depart from an order he should at once inform the issuer of it, and the Commanders of any neighbouring units likely to be affected.

I maintain that I carried out these regulations to the letter, and that had I carried out my orders to retire on the 26th, I should, under sub-paragraph iii. of above, have failed in my duties and rightly been held responsible. I submit that the circumstances which I am about to relate clearly demanded a departure from my orders.

With these circumstances of which Lord French, judging both from his despatches and book, evidently has a very hazy idea, I shall now proceed to deal.

I will first endeavour to draw attention to his inaccuracies regarding the incidents which led up to my decision to fight at Le Cateau.

Page 74, he says: "The retreat had been resumed at daybreak, and at 6 p.m. all the troops of the 2nd Corps were on the Le Cateau line, except McCracken's Brigade, which, as before described, had been obliged to stand and fight at Solesmes."

To make the story of McCracken's fight referred to more complete, I will quote again from the Field Marshal's book, page 72, "the only action of importance during the day occurred at Solesmes when the rearguard of the 3rd Division, under McCracken, was heavily attacked. Allenby with the 2nd Cavalry Brigade, 4th Dragoon Guards, 9th Lancers, 18th Hussars, came to his assistance and enabled him to continue his retreat. He did not however arrive at his appointed destination till late in the evening, and then it was with very tired men."

And again page 75:—

"Things did not go so well with the 2nd Corps. General Allenby who had been most ably covering the retreat of the Army with his Cavalry, had already materially assisted the rearguard of the 3rd Division to surmount their difficulties at Solesmes.

McCracken's Brigade (7th) 3rd Battn. Worcester Regt., 2nd Battn. S. Lancs. Regt., 1st Battn. Wilts Regt. and 2nd Battn. R. Irish Rifles, did not reach the Le Cateau position until 10 or 11 p.m. on the 25th inst. His men were of course nearly done up and he had suffered severe losses."

These descriptions by Lord French are astounding, for things had gone quite well with the 2nd Corps. The march was an abnormally long one in a very hot sun, longer than that performed by the 1st Corps. The rearguard fighting, except that at Solesmes, had not been heavy and the total casualties in the whole Corps, including the 7th Brigade, were under 100. On this day the Cavalry, 19th Brigade and 4th Division were working under orders from G.H.Q.

Now the Cavalry throughout the day had done wonders with small casualties*, in keeping the enemy at a distance from our infantry, and they helped McCracken materially in his rearguard action.

Solesmes and the road south of it were packed with the wagons of French refugees fleeing before the German advance, with the transport of our own Cavalry, 3rd Division and 19th Brigade, and with parties of French Territorials cut off in their retreat from Valenciennes; to enable them to get away, a firm front by the rearguard was necessary, and right well the 2nd Wilts and the 2nd South Lancs. of the 7th Brigade responded. But it was the Cavalry that was in difficulties, out of which they were helped by McCracken, and to make this clear I cannot do better than quote General Allenby's generous letter of the 1st November, 1914, to me, from which it is apparent that Lord French's story is not supported by facts; to show also that G.H.Q. was aware of what happened, I add a copy of my letter forwarding General Allenby's recommendations of General McCracken's services to the notice of the C.-in-C. and recommending him for promotion to the rank of Major-General, *which he was given.*†

---

Headquarters, Cavalry Corps,
1st November.

My dear Sir Horace,

On the 25th August I had the task of covering the rear of the army in its western flank during the retirement on Le Cateau. Towards nightfall a fierce attack was made on the Cavalry Division under my command and a gap was opened between the rear and flank guards. The rear of the 2nd Army Corps was then passing through the town of Solesmes, a defile, and the situation became precarious. I had, at the time, *only one‡ Regiment of Cavalry to fill the gap.* Riding to the rear of the Column, I met Brigadier General McCracken and gave him the situation. Brigadier General McCracken at once rose to the occasion. He collected what troops were near to hand and led them to a position whence they could cover the column entering the defile. At the same time he stopped and brought into action a Brigade of R.F.A. and a Howitzer Battery. This ready initiative checked the enemy,

---

*Casualties 101, of which 4th Brigade had 90 in this action about Solesmes.

†He was promoted Major-General in the next *Gazette* and antedated to 14th October, 1914.

‡Lord French has distinctly said that General Allenby with a whole Brigade enabled General McCracken to continue his retreat.

but they brought several batteries into action under whose cover their infantry resumed the attack. Until after dark Brigadier General McCracken maintained his stand under severe gun and rifle fire and did not retire until the rear of the column was in safety. He then withdrew skilfully and with comparatively few casualties. I consider that his ready and daring handling of the rearguard averted a mishap which might have been a disaster. I am glad to be able to bring his action to your notice, as I think it deserves recognition.

Yours sincerely,<br>
(Sd.) E. H. H. ALLENBY.

From
> The General Officer Commanding, 2nd Corps,

To
> The Military Secretary
> to the Commander-in-Chief.

3rd November, 1914.

Sir,

I have just received from Lt.-General Allenby, Commanding the Cavalry Corps, the attached letter, a typed copy of which I also send for easy reference. I hope you will lay it before the Commander-in-Chief and explain to him that had I been aware of Brigadier General McCracken's especially commendable services on the evening of the 25th August, at an earlier date, I should have certainly recommended—taking into consideration his other valuable services—that he be specially promoted to the rank of Major-General for service in the Field, and I still hope that it may not be too late for such recognition to be made.

(Sd.) H. L. SMITH-DORRIEN,<br>
General,<br>
Commanding 2nd Army Corps.

It must appear therefore that the Field Marshal in writing his story of 1914 has not allowed his opinions to be influenced by reports favourable to the units of the 2nd Corps, no matter from what source.

It will be noted in one of the above quotations from the Field Marshal's book he has said that *at 6 p.m. on the 25th all troops of the 2nd Corps were on the Le Cateau line except McCracken's Brigade*, and later, page 76, he says: "**McCracken's Brigade did not reach the Le Cateau position until 10 or 11 p.m. on the 25th,**" and (on page 76 and 77)

"I had late in the evening of the 25th, before leaving for my headquarters at St. Quentin, visited several units of the 2nd Corps in their bivouacs and though tired indeed they had not struck me as worn out troops—by the break of day on the 26th, the 5th Division on the right had secured several hours rest, the same may be said of the 8th and 9th Brigades which came next in the line. The 7th Brigade had only just arrived in cantonments at 10 p.m. or 11 p.m. on the 25th after a heavy day's march and some severe fighting, but they could in such an emergency have marched at dawn. The 4th Division on the left of the 2nd Corps was comparatively fresh" and then he goes on to emphasize how he visited one brigade of Artillery. I do not say he did not pay *several* visits, but I have endeavoured, without success, to ascertain what units the Field Marshal actually visited; official reports show that, beyond a few Supply Units which had started in the small hours, there were not, until late in the evening, any troops in the bivouacs and billets they occupied that night. I myself arrived in the town of Le Cateau at 3·30 p.m., and at once sought for the C.-in-C. He was not to be found either at G.H.Q. office, or at the chateau he had been living in, and no one knew when he had left or where he had gone to, not even the Chief of the Staff, Sir Archibald Murray, who was still there; the G.H.Q. was in process of being moved to St. Quentin, and it was generally believed that the C.-in-C. had gone in the direction of that place.

I shall now proceed to give details of the hours at which the several parts of the 2nd Corps reached their billets.

5TH DIVISION. From *official reports* this 5th Division was the only one which marched through Le Cateau during daylight, "*the head of it reached the town at 3 p.m., the tail of it after dark.*"

(N.B.—Sun set at 7 p.m., so it can hardly have been dark before 8.)

The bivouacs were mostly from $\frac{3}{4}$ of a mile to 2 miles to the south of the town, and it would be a conservative estimate to add $1\frac{1}{2}$ to 2 hours to those times, before units could be settled for the night.

One and a half battalions of the 14th Brigade of the 5th Division were sent back to occupy the high ground on the east of Le Cateau, so as to connect if possible with the 1st Corps, which the operation orders had led me to expect would arrive on the right or east of the 2nd Corps. I had been given no information of their having started too late to reach the Le Cateau position *as ordered,* and as the forest of Mormal intervened between the two Corps, and had been allotted to the 1st Corps in G.H.Q. Operation Order No. 7 of 25th August, it was not possible for me to keep in touch with them. These 1½ battalions had a very unsettled night, as, in common with the whole Force, they had to entrench themselves, which detracted much from the limited time available for rest.

The 28th Brigade R.F.A., which had been on rearguard, did not reach their destination at Reumont until 11·30 p.m.

No. 2 and 3 Section of 5th Divisional Ammunition Column did not reach the same place until the morning of the 26th. The 5th Division had had a hard day's fighting with 363 casualties on the 23rd, a still harder day with 1500 casualties on the 24th, and had had a most trying march of at least 20 to 25 miles along a pavé road under an almost tropical sun; all air being kept off by the forest of Mormal. It must be remembered too that the bulk of the troops were reservists totally unfit for the severe march in marching order, mostly with new boots, and that they only reached their bivouacs after over twenty hours of continuous and heavy work.

3RD DIVISION. The main columns reached their positions about 6·30 p.m., the rearguard (7th Brigade) shortly before midnight, except the 2nd Bn. Royal Irish Rifles, part of the South Lancashires and 41st Battalion R.F.A.; these were cut off in the roads crowded with fugitives and French Territorials and did not reach Maurois until 4 a.m. on the 26th and only got back to their Division about 8 a.m.*

The conditions and hardships described for the 5th Division apply in a slightly less degree to the 3rd Division, but it was very late before they all got settled for the night and all were very weary. The total casualties in the 3rd Division for the 23rd, 24th and 25th August were 2084, excluding stragglers.

4TH DIVISION. Under the orders from G.H.Q. this Division had been sent forward to the neighbourhood of Briastre to cover the retirement of the 3rd Division, the Cavalry Division, and 19th Brigade, with orders to remain out until all were through. This is supported by

(1) a message from General Snow to Sir A. Murray dated Point 129 S.W. of Viesly, 5·55 p.m. 25th August, saying that he had at last got into touch with the 19th Brigade and believed they were at St. Hilaire (4 miles N.W. of Viesly) and asking for orders, and

(2) the following message from G.H.Q. evidently in reply to (1): "*You are quite right, you must remain out until the 19th Brigade and Cavalry Division set in. Have you any news of the*

---
*Authority—War Diaries and Maurice, D.A.A.G. 3rd Division.

*Cavalry? We have none. The 2nd Corps are in their appointed places and the 1st Corps are also all right about Landrecies. The present intention is to continue the retirement to-morrow, you (with 19th Brigade attached) to start first at 7 a.m. Use Bowes to send in to the Cavalry if you want him."*

(N.B.—This order attaches the 19th Brigade to the 4th Division; the Brigade had been placed under orders of the 2nd Corps, (G.H.Q. O.O.S. of 25th August, 1 p.m.)

It was not until 6·10 p.m. that they got into touch with the last two, and their G.O.C.'s (Major General Snow) report says: *" Owing to the amount of transport of Cavalry Division and 3rd Division which passed through Viesly, the movement of the rearguard of the 4th Division was delayed until after midnight—the result was that the three Brigades did not get on to the position till about daylight, that is, between 3·30 and 5·30 a.m. on the 26th."*

This unquestionable evidence disposes of the Field Marshal's statement that the 4th Division could be very fresh.

Lord French, judging from his self-discredited official despatch of the 7th September, 1914, appears to have been under the delusion that he had placed the 4th Division under my orders, but this was not the case until later; the fact that this was so is proved by that Division's having reported to and received all its instructions from G.H.Q. until the 26th, when General Snow agreed to take orders from me. It appears, though, that the 4th Division had been told to be prepared to help me, if called on, for at 7·45 a.m. on August 25th, the G.O.C. of that Division despatched the following message to G.O.C. 2nd Corps :—*" have been ordered by G.H.Q. to report to you in order to assist you if you require it, G.G. 3."* (Authority—Major Becke's, " Royal Regiment of Artillery at Le Cateau " (page 5).

To quote from General Snow's report on the Battle of Le Cateau *" 1st phase, 5·30 a.m. to 10 a.m. (26th August).*

*(13). It is first necessary to state that about 5·30 a.m. when op. orders were being issued from Division H.Q. at Haucourt to carry out the retirement laid down in op. order No. 8 of 7 p.m. of the 25th from G.H.Q. and O.A. 304/26th received at 5·28 a.m. 26th August, a message was received from the 2nd Corps to say that it could not retire and it was going to fight on its present position and asking the 4th Division to protect its left flank as far as Haucourt.*

*(14). A repy lwas at once sent to say the 4th Division would at once comply and General Bowes, a representative of G.S. at G.H.Q., then with the 4th Division was informed of the decision. The 4th Division then came under command of G.O.C. 2nd* **Army Corps."**

A further message sent to General Snow and received by him at 7·20 a.m. on the 26th August reads as follows:—

"*To 4th Division G.W. 1, August 26th—from information received from the Cavalry it has been found necessary to remain in our present position. The 2nd Corps is taking up a position from Reumont-Troisvilles-Audencourt-Caudry Station. Sir Horace Smith-Dorrien hopes that you will hold the ground on his left as far as Haucourt.*"

The Staff diary 2nd Corps has this entry: "*5 a.m., 26th August. A Staff Officer (Capt. Walcot) sent to 4th Division to say that Commander of 2nd Corps had assumed command of all troops in the area of battle, and ordering 4th Division to prolong the line to west with left thrown back from Caudry (exclusive) to neighbourhood of Haucourt (inclusive).*"

Again the following is an extract from a message from C.-in-C. to me, *i.e.*, 2nd Corps: "*O.A. 307, 11 a.m., 26th August, '4th Division must co-operate with you.'*"

I now come to one of the most important of the F.M.'s mis-statements regarding myself, on page 76.

Talking of the report Colonel Ansell made to General Allenby about 2 a.m. regarding the German advance he says: "This seemed of such great importance that the latter at once sought out Sir Horace Smith-Dorrien, and warned him that unless he was prepared to continue his march *at daybreak* he would most probably be pinned down to his position and be unable to get away. Sir Horace asked General Allenby what in his opinion were the chances he had if he remained and held the position, adding that he felt convinced his troops were so exhausted as to preclude the possibility of removing them for some hours to come. Allenby's reply was that he thought unless the Commander of the 2nd Corps made up his mind to move *at daylight*, the enemy would probably succeed in surrounding him—nevertheless Sir Horace Smith-Dorrien determined to fight.

As to this decision, a Commander on the spot, and in close touch with his Divisions and Brigades is in the best position to judge of what his men can do."

Now the last paragraph really governs the question, and it is evident from what he has said that the F.M., 4 to 5 years after the event was ignorant of what I learnt on that eventful morn. I have already quoted the F.S. Regulations which justify, *nay, insist on*, a Commander departing from his orders under special circumstances.

That there was any question of my not intending to carry out his orders to continue the retreat, there can be no doubt. 2nd Corps orders and Divisional orders all bear this out, and the change of order to stand and fight which reached the Divisions about 5 a.m. on the 26th came as a surprise to them. I have already shown that, so far from all the troops being on the Le Cateau line by 6 p.m. as the F.M. states (page 74), far more than one third of them were on the move all night and got no rest at all; I am sure that when he appreciates this, he will realise that the Commander on the spot could hardly have expected them to march on *at daylight*, but according to what General Allenby really said, *daylight would be too late*. It was about 2 a.m. on the 26th when General Allenby came to my Headquarters at Bertry. He told me his troops were much scattered, 2½ Brigades being at Catillon, 6 miles east of Le Cateau and 1½ at Vièsle*, and further that he was at a loss what to do as his men and horses were tired and he could not get into touch with G.H.Q. (under whose direct orders he was). He further said that if *I could not march on at once (in the dark)* the Germans were so close that I would be forced to fight *at daylight*. This is confirmed by the following letters, which he has sent me:—

My Dear General,                                                   4th June, 1919.

In reply to your letter of the 8th May:—I have not seen any part of Lord French's book as yet. I remember the Conference at Compiègne, but I have no recollection of your expressing an opinion to the effect that the only course open was to return to the Base, re-embark and land elsewhere. As regards Le Cateau, you fought there *in consequence* of the report I made to you. I said that *unless your troops could resume their retreat before daylight* it would be in my opinion impossible to extricate them. You consulted with Hubert Hamilton and Forestier Walker, and they reported the troops could not continue their retreat during the hours of the darkness. You therefore decided to stand and fight. I think you only had those two alternatives—to march on during the night, or to fight.

        With all good wishes,

            Yours sincerely,

                    (Sd.) EDMUND H. ALLENBY.

---

*Sir J. F. in his official despatch of 7th September, 1914, says: "During the fighting on the 24th and 25th the Cavalry became a good deal scattered, but by the early morning of the 26th, General Allenby had succeeded in concentrating the Brigades to the *south of Cambrai.*"

I am afraid this description would hardly be accurate enough for an official history as Vièsle and Catillon, near which places the Cavalry Brigade actually were, are respectively 10 and 20 miles east of Cambrai.

The Residency, CAIRO,
15th June, 1919.

My Dear General,

Yours of the 30th May. I have read the newspaper cutting you enclose. You will have had my reply to your letter of the 8th May. My recollection of what I said to you when I came to your H.Q. is that if your troops could not recommence their march in retreat *before daylight* they could not get away, as the Germans were close on their billets; and that, in that case, *it would be necessary to fight.*

When you asked me if I would act under your orders, if you decided to fight a delaying action, I agreed.

I remember that you sent for Hubert Hamilton and asked him if his men could march on, and, as far as I remember, he said they could not *march before 9 a.m.*

Yours sincerely,
(Sd.) EDMUND H. ALLENBY.

---

My Dear General,                    13th July, 1919.

Yours of 22nd June with enclosures. I have received and answered your letters of the 8th and 30th of May. The latter of them I answered on the 15th June as I have said. I remember no counsel of despair coming from you at Compiègne on the 29th August. On the night of 25th-26th August, I came to your H.Q. and gave you the situation as I knew it. I said that unless your troops could march on *before daylight*, they would not be able to continue their retreat, the Germans being too close. You consulted Hubert Hamilton and Forestier Walker, and they reported that *it was not possible to get on the move during the hours of darkness. You then asked me if I would act under your orders if you decided to fight and I agreed to do so readily.*

Yours sincerely,
(Sd.) EDMUND H. ALLENBY.

---

The Residency, CAIRO,
RAMLEH,

Dear General,                    25/7/19.

Yours of the 29th June—certainly quote my letters as you suggest, &c., &c.

Yours sincerely,
(Sd.) EDMUND H. ALLENBY.

G.H.Q.,
E.E.F.,
CAIRO, 11/10/19.

My Dear General,

In reply to your letter of the 27th September, I am sorry that I have not time to take part in the controversy. I have no objection, however, to your publishing any of the letters I have written to you on the matters to which you refer.

Sincerely yours,
(Sd.) EDMUND H. ALLENBY.

---

I then held a Conference to ascertain the state of all troops.

Present:—G.O.C. 2nd Corps General Smith-Dorrien and his G.S.O. 1 B.G. Forestier Walker, G.O.C. Cavalry Division Lieut.-General Allenby and his G.S.O., 1 Colonel J. Vaughan, and D.A.A.G. Major Macalpine Leny, G.O.C. 3rd Division Major-General Hubert Hamilton (killed 14th October, 1914).

General Hamilton said his troops could not possibly move before 9 a.m. (Generals Allenby and Maurice (who was on General Hamilton's Staff), both support this statement) and in any case it would be impossible to set them going *before daylight*. The 5th Division were in even a worse plight, being more scattered, the 4th Division were, as I have already shown, still out when the Conference was held, and their return was uncertain; the Cavalry were very scattered and exhausted; the roads were encumbered with transport and refugees in carts and on foot.

After considering these points, I appreciated that any attempt to retire without striking a blow was impossible.

The following are the arguments which passed through my mind :—

(a) It must be long after daylight before a rearward march along the whole front could be commenced.

(b) The enemy were in force close to our billets.

(c) To turn our backs on them in broad daylight with worn out men suffering from sore feet, would leave the latter a prey to enemy cavalry supported by infantry in motors.

(d) The roads were encumbered with civilian fugitives and country carts, as well as with the transport belonging to the Force, some of which was still on the enemy side of our position, and time to allow them to clear off was essential.

(*e*) The last news of the 1st Corps was that it was fighting hard some miles to the N.E. of us, and that, were we to retire, its left flank would be exposed to the full brunt of Von Kluck's troops.

(N.B.—That the F.M. realised that the 2nd Corps covered the left flank of the 1st Corps, is apparent from his word painting, on page 78, quoted later.)

(*f*) I had gained great confidence in the shooting power of our Infantry, since I had seen them mow down the German hordes at Mons. I knew that I could rely on our gunners, and that if General Allenby would act under me and General Sordet with the 1st French Cavalry Corps would guard my left, I had splendid Cavalry on both flanks.

(*g*) In view of the foregoing I had every reason to hope that we should be successful in giving the Germans a stopping blow, under cover of which we might be able to retire.

(*h*) Finally with the enemy in force close to our billets the only hope of withdrawing successfully was to strike a blow first and to retire under the confusion caused by that blow.

What my personal feelings were can best be judged by a conversation I had on the telephone at 7 a.m. on the 26th. About 6·45 a message was brought to my headquarters at Bertry saying the C.-in-C. wished to speak to me on the telephone (by the railway wire between St. Quentin and Bertry Station). My Headquarters was about ½ mile from the latter, and jumping into a motor I went there and called up G.H.Q. and was answered by the Assistant Chief of Staff, General Sir Henry Wilson, on behalf of the C.-in-C. I explained the situation and that the battle had already begun. General Wilson told me that Sir John did not wish me to fight and that I was to break off the action as soon as possible, and continue retiring. I told him I was quite hopeful of being able to deal the enemy a smashing blow, and if things went right, would fight until dark and slip away; he replied wishing me good luck, emphasising that I should retire as soon as possible, and remarking that mine was the first cheerful voice he had heard for 3 days.

When I said I would stand and fight, if Allenby would act under my orders, and he agreed, there was an evident air of relief amongst those present at the Conference. A message was at once sent to General Sordet, Commanding the 1st French Cavalry Corps, asking him to protect my west or left flank. G.H.Q. was also informed.

This appears to me a suitable place to insert a paper I have received from Major-General Sir G. Forestier Walker—regarding the Conference at Bertry—as he was present in his capacity of B.G.G.S. 2nd Corps; his statement is of special value.

## THE BATTLE OF LE CATEAU.
### Statement by Major-General G. T. Forestier Walker.

*1. During the whole of the period covered by the retreat from MONS I was B.G.G.S. of the 2nd Corps.*

*2. At about 2 a.m. on the 26th, General Allenby arrived at 2nd Corps H.Q. and interviewed the Corps Commander. I was present during the whole of the interview.*

*General Allenby described the positions of his troops so far as he knew them, and stated that they were very exhausted. He also gave later information as to the progress made by the enemy that had until then been received by the 2nd Corps, especially as regards its threat to the left flank of the British. He expressed the strong opinion that, unless the Corps was to incur the risk of being pinned to the ground, the units should be put in march with the least possible delay, and should be clear of the position before it was light enough for the enemy to attack.*

*3. It was manifestly impossible to carry out this suggestion. Some of the units had only reached the position by midnight or later, and some had not been reported "in" at the time of this interview.*

*All the Infantry of the 3rd and 5th Divisions were very exhausted, and would be slow in getting on the move.*

*As B.G.G.S., I pointed out to the Corps Commander that a change in orders could not possibly reach the smaller units, under the circumstances, without considerable delay, and that it would be impossible at that late hour to get the tired troops on the march, much less clear of the position, before daylight. It was a question, therefore, whether to adhere to the orders previously issued, or to do the best in the time at our disposal to perfect the defensive arrangements which had been already begun the day before, and to accept battle.*

*The decision of the Corps Commander was prompt and definite, to accept battle.*

*4. I cannot now remember to what extent, if any, the Corps Commander discussed the pros and cons, but the opinion of my-*

*self and the other members of the Staff was, and in my own case still is, as follows:—*

*If, as appeared certain from General Allenby's information, the enemy attack should catch the Corps in front (i.e., normal front) and flank in the act of moving off, the result would almost certainly be disastrous to us.*

*On the other hand, there was every prospect of our being able to put up a good fight by holding the ground on which we stood. The enemy would be bound to suffer terribly, and there was a fair prospect that we could hold him off until night and then continue our march, knowing that he would be in no position to pursue.*

*At the worst, we could with confidence count on checking the enemy to such an extent as to ensure the safety of the 1st Corps.*

G. FORESTIER WALKER,

Wilton, 3/8/19.             Major-General.

My B.G.G.S. drafted and issued orders for a delaying action, including full instructions for retirement, the latter only to be acted on when I gave the order, and the battle was fought, resulting in such a heavy blow to the enemy that the subsequent retirement of the British Army was never seriously interfered with.

In support of this I quoted from Sir J. F.'s despatch of 7th September, 1914, "**fortunately the enemy had himself suffered too heavily to engage in energetic pursuit.**"

It is true that Lord French has now repudiated certain parts of the despatch in question, but as the sentence I have quoted was not amongst them, I conclude that, in this matter, 5 years' consideration has not altered his opinion formed when events were fresh in his mind.

In this connection I would also quote from Major A. F. Becke's carefully considered book, "The Royal Artillery at Le Cateau," written 5 years after the events he describes, and based entirely on official records, and a mass of undeniable evidence which he has taken enormous trouble to collect.

*" On the 26th August, 1914, the most powerful and best equipped fighting machine ever put into the field up to that time, flushed too with the joy of a campaign successfully opened, had been opposed in a bitter fight by a force of half its strength that stood undauntedly at bay to bar its further onrush. By the end of that day the attackers had been beaten to a standstill, and so mauled that their only desire was to allow the 2nd Corps to continue its withdrawal from the field unmolested, save by sullen boom*

*of the German guns; and their unsupported fire at this moment was the sure proof of the discomfiture suffered by the German host.*

*For four days the pressure and pursuit had been those of an army, a conquering army. But the action of Le Cateau, fought on the 26th August, 1914, changed the character of the pursuit of the German army and thereafter it degenerated into a respectful pursuit by mounted troops and mobile detachments only."*

My knowledge of Major Becke is merely that gained by reading his book, and this it is impossible to do without being impressed with the view that never has the British Artillery been more skilfully handled, and never has a Force in retirement shown a higher fighting spirit, or been *more* convinced that they had dealt the enemy a staggering blow.

I would mention too, that, although up till now we have not had much information from the Germans as to how they regard the Battle of Le Cateau, what we have had does not indicate at any rate that they regard it as a knock out blow for the British.

General Von Zwehl, formerly Commanding 7th Reserve Corps, in a criticism on Lord French's book, says that on the 26th August, 1914, the Germans only claimed 2,600 prisoners, and usually their figures include wounded and possible dead.

I must emphasise here that had my right flank not been turned, I should have had no difficulty about holding my ground until dark, as I originally intended.

Both the 3rd and 4th Divisions were full of confidence, and much annoyed when my order reached them to carry out my pre-arranged plan of retirement. The following is a message sent by the 4th Division at 1.35 p.m. from La Mottee :—

*A.M., 26th.—Situation much as described in my A.M., 23rd. All Brigades holding their own well. 12th Brigade has advanced and is re-occupying ground occupied this morning. No attack from west, but strong attack from north-west this morning which was at first successful, but was driven back by counter-attack of Royal Irish Fusiliers. I have sent Colonel Edmonds to explain the situation, but at present I see no need of or advantage in retiring. I must feed my men this evening, they have fought splendidly to-day, but are very hungry and exhausted, and I consider a further retirement may damp their now excellent spirits. I believe 4th Cavalry Brigade to be at Walmcourt."*

I have given quite a clear account of the actual incidents which caused me to issue the order to retire, in the entry of the 26th August in my diary in Appendix " A."

There it will be seen that the deciding factor was a message from the G.O.C. 5th Division saying his men were showing signs of wavering. This message was brought to me by Colonel (now Major-General) the Honourable F. Gathorne Hardy, and I at once sent him to General Sir Charles Ferguson's Headquarters at Reumont to order an organized retirement, as the sure means of steadying the troops. Colonel Gathorne Hardy was to say at the same time that I would order the other Divisions to conform, *i.e.*, cover their retirement and then retire themselves.

I must admit that I am puzzled with the next statement on page 77, which Lord French appears to believe, for it entirely discredits General Allenby's serious estimate of the numbers and proximity of the enemy on the night of the 25th. It reads as follows:—

"**All reconnaissances and intelligence reports received up to midnight on the 25th, concur in saying that Cambrai was then still in the position of the French, and that the position there was not yet seriously threatened, further, that whilst there were clear signs of the outflanking movements in progress, no considerable bodies of the enemy had yet crossed the line Valenciennes-Douai, and that after their repulse at Solesmes by McCracken and Allenby, the enemy was not in strength south of the line Valenciennes-Maubeuge.**"

Remember that Lord French has denounced me for my decision to fight, which I came to in view of the serious news given me by General Allenby of the enemy in strength close to my billets, and that within a few paragraphs he makes a further statement that his own information was to the effect that no large body of the enemy was within 20 miles of me, *i.e.*, south of the line Valenciennes-Maubeuge.

If this was really the case, which it was not*, where was the risk I took in standing to fight a rear-guard action to rest my troops? Or is it his intention to imply that, as the enemy were in no strength at Le Cateau, the task of keeping them off was not a great one?

Page 77.—The Field Marshal says after his above reference to the 2nd Corps: "**The 1st Corps had as we know experienced a much harder day's march on the 25th, and was attacked at Landrecies and its neighbourhood before it could get any rest at all.**" But surely the 2nd Corps had

---

*Von Kluck's own statement of his dispositions on the night of the 25th, given later, bears out General Allenby's report to me of about 2 a.m. on the 26th.

marched considerably further, for they reached the line ordered, whereas Sir John says himself (page 74) that the 1st Corps had started late, and had had to halt some miles short of the allotted position.

(N.B.—Landrecies is some 7 or 8 miles short of Le Cateau. A reference to the Map is suggested.)

Had the 1st Corps marched in accordance with their orders, the engagement at Landrecies, in which the 4th Guards Brigade so distinguished themselves late at night, would never have been fought.

I mention this to emphasize that Lord French words his statements in such a manner as to get the public to believe that the 1st Corps could do nothing wrong, whereas the 2nd Corps could do nothing right.

Page 78.—The Field Marshal says "the superb gallantry of the troops and the skilful leading of divisional and brigade and battalion Commanders, helped very materially by the support given by Allenby, and, as I afterwards learned, by Sordet and D'Amade, saved the 2nd Corps, which otherwise would assuredly been pinned to their ground and then surrounded.

The Cavalry might have made good their retreat, but 3 out of 5 Divisions of the British Army with the 7th Brigade *(presumably he means the 19th)* must have been lost. The enemy, flushed by this primary victory, would have pressed in on the flanks of the 1st Corps, cut off their retreat and a stupendous repetition of Sedan might well have resulted."

Surely this pessimistic summary is hardly warranted, since the Field Marshal on the previous page (77) told us that up to midnight on the 25th there were no Germans in strength within 20 miles of the Le Cateau position, and that the estimate was confirmed by a German wireless message on the evening of the 26th August.

That his appreciation was at fault is beside the question; that it was at fault is proved by Von Kluck's own statement of his dispositions on the evening of the 25th August, according to which he had one whole Corps (the 4th) and two Cavalry Divisions immediately in touch with my troops, the heads of another Corps (2nd) in two columns within 8 miles of my left, one Division of the 3rd Corps within 6 miles of my right, and two more Corps within 6 hours march of the battle-field.

But why did not this terrible fate befall the B.E.F., and why does an army ever go into battle without being forced to surrender? I submit that the very words of the Field Marshal supply the answer, namely, bravery of troops, skill of subordinate leaders, mutual support given by Cavalry, in fact everything an army is trained for—and everything I had when I accepted battle.

Curiously enough Mr. Lovat Fraser in a vigorous and hostile article (Appendix " C ") in the *Weekly Dispatch* of 25th February, 1917, attacks me for having fought the action; from what he says, it is evident that he was under the same impressions regarding the situation as Lord French when he wrote " 1914," but it is interesting to note that as far as the actual handling of the troops is concerned he gives me great praise for he says: *" the Battle of Le Cateau was no disaster and for this General Smith-Dorrien deserves full credit. It is generally admitted that he showed great skill and coolness in extricating his badly hammered forces when he broke off the battle early in the afternoon."*

I do not argue that I am entitled to as great praise as Mr. Fraser has given me, but I submit that, if a hostile critic can express such views, and if it is considered, after studying the true facts as set forth in this paper, that I was justified in fighting, then that I am entitled not only to be publicly cleared of the Field Marshal's charges, but to be granted some credit for the unavoidable Battle of Le Cateau.

I ask, is this blood curdling picture likening the possible disaster to Sedan relevant, considering what actually happened? There was no question of a disaster, and this Mr. Lovat Fraser, has made clear. I gathered at the time that the C.-in-C. was perturbed, but I feel bound to defend him from himself, for I saw no signs then of his being as unhinged as might appear from this harrowing and imaginary description written so long after the events.

Now as Commander at Le Cateau it is very gratifying to me to see that the Field Marshal appreciates the magnificent leadership and fighting spirit shown by everyone except the Commander, and I sympathise with all who fought under me that day if it is a fact that their chief leader was not worthy of them, but I owe it to the other arms to publish a letter received from the G.S.O. 1 of the Cavalry Division Colonel (now Brigadier General) John Vaughan, which is as follows :—

*ANGLESEY HOUSE,*
*ALDERSHOT,*
*24/6/19.*

My Dear Sir Horace,

*I have just received your letter of 14th inst.*

*I remember accompanying General Allenby when we visited your H.Q. at Bertry. I also remember the situation as it* appeared at the time to Allenby and me; your setting forth the reasons which determined you to fight, and the fact that Allenby thought you were right in doing so. <u>In fact both Allenby and I were much relieved that you had determined to fight as, inter alia, it gave us a chance of getting hold of our scattered brigades again.</u>

I also remember the action of the French Cavalry under Sordet, who emerged from Cambrai and attacked the German right in the evening.

To my mind this was a very opportune action on Sordet's part as he had got outside the German flank—and their subsequent advance gave us (British Cavalry) no trouble at all. Prior to your action at Le Cateau the German Cavalry outflanked us via Tournai and Denain and was a very serious menace.

Feeling, most strongly as I do, that it was your action at Le Cateau combined with Sordet's outflanking move that made the rest of our retreat possible and easy I should certainly wish to give any evidence I can in support of this theory.

From the British Cavalry point of view I consider that the Huns gave us no trouble at all after Le Cateau, as we were always able to fight delaying actions and retire at our leisure, once the German outflanking movement had petered out.

I am quite sure that the above is also Allenby's views.

I have a series of lectures on Cavalry actions which I prepared during the war, for the purpose of educating our new officers in France. Included in this are most of our actions during the retreat. I also went to both the Bertry and Mons battlefields either just before or after the armistice, and I personally am convinced that if you had'nt fought at Le Cateau, you might have got your infantry away <u>but you would have lost all your transport.</u>

I have met no officer in this country who does not deprecate Lord French's action in writing his story of 1914. Every one had difficulties to cope with then, and I am not aware that we received much assistance from G.H.Q. at the time, in fact we received none, nor any orders for that matter, <u>except verbal ones which could be repudiated if necessary. Gough, Walker and I had to go to G.H.Q. at night to get these.</u>

There is one slight inaccuracy in what you say took place, " viz., Allenby said he had $2\frac{1}{2}$ Brigades about Catillon and $1\frac{1}{2}$ Brigades about Caudry and Ligny." For the latter it should be " $1\frac{1}{2}$ Brigades about Viesly." The point is perhaps worth noting, because it shows your flank as being more exposed than *if you place the Brigades at Caudry and Ligny. We marched west past those places at dawn next morning to a position of readiness near Honnecourt, I think, where we watched your left flank and got touch with Sordet towards Cambrai.*

*You are at liberty to make use of any of these statements and I should be glad to give evidence in this sense before any court of enquiry.*

Yours sincerely,<br>(Sd.) JOHN VAUGHAN.

No one after reading this could claim that the 3 Divisions and 19th Brigade were saved by the Cavalry.

It is too a very open question whether General D'Amade's troops were near enough to exercise any influence on the course of the battle. I never received any definite report of their action, and according to the "Journal d'un Officier de Cavalerie," by Charles Vernazobres, p. 30, the French Territorial Divisions left Cambrai for Arras and Bapaume early in the morning of the 26th. If this is correct, since those places are respectively about 20 miles N.W. and S.W. of Cambrai it is evident they cannot have taken much part in the battle of Le Cateau—especially as the left flank of the British troops was at Esnes, 6 miles on the east or opposite side of Cambrai.

Curiously enough the only report I received about them was one at 6˙55 a.m. on 26th (vide II. Corps' diary):—

"Information received that 2 French Divisions are marching from Arras and Peronne" but I never got anything further, and it is possible the troops reported were really going away from Cambrai; if so this would confirm the report of the French Cavalry Officer and would account for my hearing no more of them.

This however the French authorities should be able to clear up.

That I recognised the great assistance given by General Sordet I have already shown in the Order of the Day I issued on the 29th August, 1914.

I issued that order because, as I recount later, I realised that General Sordet had loyally complied with my request to guard my left flank—but I had no information as to the nature of the fighting which had fallen to the lot of the French Cavalry that day. An interesting book has just appeared* which indicates that their action was confined to an artillery duel.

---

*"Trois mois au Premier Corps de Cavalerie—Par E. Letard, Veterinaire Aide-Major au 3ᵉ. Hussards." Paris: Plon-Nourrit, Nov. 1919.

The book relates how on the evening of the 25th the 3rd Division of Sordet's Cavalry was at Aubancheul, 8 miles S.W. of the British left in the coming battle. Next morning it advanced towards Cambrai, hearing the sounds of the battle and expecting to use the arme blanche, but after long expectancy, came in the afternoon under the fire of the German guns and replied with the French's 75's, continuing its retirement to Heudicourt half way between Cambrai and Peronne late in the afternoon.

The Field Marshal states, p. 78, that he only heard afterwards of General Sordet's help, but I am inclined to think that after 4 or 5 years of strenuous work he has forgotten the facts which are as follows :—

In addition to sending a special message to General Sordet in the small hours of the 26th August, telling him I was going to fight, and asking him to guard my left flank, I had wired to G.H.Q. as follows :—

"5 a.m., August 26th—2nd Corps to G.H.Q.

"G. 368, Inform French Cavalry Corps that 2nd Corps is "not retiring to-day, and ask for their co-operation on our "left flank."

About 4 p.m. on 26th, when riding with the troops returning through the village of Maretz, I heard very heavy gun fire out west, and, fearing that the Germans were working round between Cambrai and the left of Snow's Division, I galloped to some high ground in the direction of the firing, and then it was that I was relieved to recognise the firing from its sharpness and rapidity as that of the French Artillery, and rode back satisfied that General Sordet was there.

Next morning at my temporary Headquarters in the Mairie at St. Quentin there arrived a Staff Officer from General Sordet who described the fighting of the French Cavalry.

I was on the verge of writing to thank General Sordet, when it struck me that his leadership had been of such importance as to point to his receiving the thanks of the British C.-in-C., through General Joffre. I therefore sent my verbal thanks, wrote out the Order of the Day I have already quoted as issued on 29th August, and wrote a despatch (which I sent off by motor cyclist about 11 a.m. on the 29th August) to Sir John French. In this despatch I spoke of the helpful work of Sordet's Cavalry on my exposed flank and asked that the C.-in-C.'s thanks might be conveyed to General Sordet through the French C.-in-C.

About the following October or November when my Headquarters were at Baileul, Sir J. French's despatch of the

7th September 1914 was published, and I was aghast to read the following regarding General Sordet :—

"Although he rendered me valuable assistance later on in the course of the retirement, he was unable for the reasons given to afford me any support on the most critical day of all, viz., the 26th."

I took the first opportunity of going into G.H.Q. at St. Omer to point out that there was evidently a clerical error as to dates, but this the C.-in-C. would not admit, asserting that he had better evidence than I had, and that I was the person who was wrong as to dates. I then told him the whole story, as recited in these papers, of General Sordet's help, and implored Sir John French to correct the matter, as in the case of an ally it was doubly necessary to be accurate and just. This he absolutely refused to do, and I left with the impression that he was using General Sordet as a scapegoat.

Some of my Staff can confirm my indignation when I returned to my own Headquarters.

So long as I remained on full pay I could do nothing to clear General Sordet of the false accusation in Sir John French's despatch.

At the end of 1916 or in January, 1917, I received a letter from General Sordet, saying that he had seen a copy of my Order of the day of 29th August, 1914, in a book by Major Corbett Smith (who was with the 2nd Corps in its retreat), and asking me for corroboration. I was then on half pay, and I wrote and told him that the order was quite genuine and further that he was at liberty to use my letter for opening the subject with the British War Office. This I believe he did, for on 24th February, 1917, I, under instructions from the Secretary of State, Lord Derby, went to the War Office on the subject of the "Interview" published in the *Weekly Dispatch* the previous Sunday (Appendix "B,") and there met Lord French in Lord Derby's presence. He told me, without my mentioning the subject, that he had admitted that Sordet had helped me at Le Cateau.

Lord French was most cordial in his manner to me and said he would never forget how indebted he was to me for my services under him in France.

It is evident Mr. Lovat Fraser did not believe that the public were aware that the amende honourable had been made, for next morning (the 25th February, 1917), the article, to which I have already referred, from his pen appeared, adversely criticising me for fighting at Le Cateau and pointing out that Sir J. French was wrong in his despatch of September 1914, as "*Sordet was spurring hard for the field in the afternoon of the 26th, and it was probably the menace which he and D'Amade were offering which saved the 2nd Corps from pursuit. The date of Lord French's despatch shows that it must have been hurriedly written at the time of the battle of the Marne and, doubtless, full reports have not been received. It may be hoped that future chroniclers will do justice to General Sordet and his Cavalry.*"

Mr. Lovat Fraser's hope has been fulfilled, for Lord French himself, after leaving General Sordet under a cloud, as far as the public are concerned, for nearly 5 years, has painted him as the true hero of the piece.

For those who are fond of diagnosis, I recommend a comparison of the ideas, suggestions and arguments in Mr. Lovat Fraser's article, above referred to, with the Field Marshal's book published two years later, for there is an extraordinary family likeness between them. The article is printed as Appendix "C."

On page 78 the Field Marshal says regarding the battle of Le Cateau :—"**The actual result was a total loss of at least 14,000 officers and men, and 80 guns.**"

Now why did he make this unwarrantable statement except to support his argument that the losses at Le Cateau were the only ones which crippled his subsequent movements?

This is a convenient place to deal also with his statement on page 87 :—

"**It was during Friday, the 28th, that I fully realised the heavy losses we had incurred since Sunday, the 23rd. These had reached in officers and men the total of upwards of 15,000, &c., &c., roughly some 60 guns, &c., &c.**

Therefore the total casualties at other actions since the campaign opened only amounted to 1,000 officers and men and no guns.

The true casualties at Le Cateau taken from official reports are as follows :—

| | |
|---|---|
| Cavalry | 5 |
| R.F.A. | 225 |
| 19th Brigade | 477 |
| 3rd Division | 1,767 (1663) |
| 5th Division | 2,248 |
| 4th Division | 3,069 |

Total 7,791.—*104* = *7687*

A great number of the casualties at Le Cateau were due to orders for the retirement not reaching units, and their being eventually surrounded and forced to surrender, as, for instance, the Gordon Highlanders.

I would also call attention to the large percentage of loss in the 4th Division, and in explanation will mention that General Snow's report described how handicapped the Division was, as it was caught in the act of concentrating, and, when it fought, had only 3 Brigades of Infantry and 4 Brigades of Artillery, without any of the following :—

>Signal Company.
>Divisional Cavalry.
>Divisional Cyclists.
>Field Ambulances.
>Field Companies, R.E.
>Train and Divisional Ammunition Column.

Now to fight a general action without any of the above auxiliary services was bound to lead to inefficiency, confusion, and heavy casualties, and I consider it most creditable to all ranks from the G.O.C. down that they fought the successful action they did.

I have already pointed out that the Division was not under my orders, but that I had merely been given permission to call on it for help.

It is obvious that with no means of communication, no engineers to assist in making defences, no ammunition column and no field ambulances to remove the wounded, the casualties in a serious battle were likely to be very large.

Undoubtedly very large numbers of wounded and stragglers who would have been taken off the field in ambulances and on ammunition and other wagons, fell into the hands of the enemy and very materially increased the total losses.

In any case the total casualties in the B.E.F. for the whole of August 1914, given by the Records Department, of killed, wounded and missing, is as follows :—

>471 officers, 13,938 other ranks—Total 14,409.

*So it is evident that not much more than half the losses which Lord French says forced him to retire, were due to me at Le Cateau, and that the losses of the 2nd Corps at Mons and Le Cateau were about the same.*

Regarding the 80 guns Lord French says I lost at Le Cateau, the official figures are 36, made up as follows :—

| | | |
|---|---|---|
| 34 | .......................... | 18 pounders. |
| 1 | .......................... | 4·5" howitzer. |
| 1 | .......................... | 60 pounder. |
| 36 | | |

It is interesting to note that the R.F.A. in personnel only had 225 casualties at Le Cateau.

On pages 79 and 80 the Field Marshal pleads that his despatch was written in a hurry during the Battle of the Marne (a statement which is in accord with Mr. Lovat Fraser's article) of 25th February, 1917, Appendix " C ") that he had no knowledge when he wrote it, of General Sordet's help at Le Cateau, and that it was based on the estimates made by the Commander of the 2nd Corps.

This implies that I gave an exaggerated account of the action generally, and was so grasping of credit and so ungenerous as to have remained silent regarding General Sordet's action. Whether this statement of the Field Marshal is justified I will leave to the judgment of those who have read what I have already said on the subject.

Why I did not refer to being helped by the Territorial Divisions under General D'Amade was because I was, and still am, in ignorance of the part they took.

I should mention that copies of Corps orders are always sent to the C.-in-C. so that in addition to my despatch asking him to thank General Sordet, addressed to him personally, a copy of my order of the day of 29th August, eulogising the French Cavalry and their Commander, was available for reference at G.H.Q.

On page 80 he defends himself and his staff from ever having given a tacit consent to the battle of Le Cateau. I have never claimed that any such consent was ever asked for or given. In an emergency a subordinate Commander has, when time does not admit of reference to his chief, to act on his own judgment and report (vide Field Service Regulations already quoted).

On the same page (80) he argues that the C.-in-C. himself is the only person who should collect the material for the compilation of a despatch, but I feel sure that in this matter he is not following the example set him by other great Commanders, and that had he allowed others to do the spade work, he would have avoided many of his inaccuracies and many of his injustices.

Chapter 5, page 81.—" A gap of some 8 miles existed between the right of the 2nd Corps at Le Cateau and the left of the 1st Corps at Landrecies."

I am not disputing this point, and I am aware that the awkward shape and position of the forest of Mormal* made it imperative that there should be *during the march* of the 25th August a considerable gap between the 1st and 2nd Corps—but it would have been interesting, if besides giving high praise to the 1st Corps, (page 82), for its skill and efficiency in contrast to his deprecating attitude towards the 2nd Corps, he had explained why the gap occurred; it was evidently no fault of the 2nd Corps, which had carried out the C.-in-C.'s orders to the letter on the 25th, and reached the destination allotted to it in its operation Order of the previous evening.

Page 82.—" It was not until 8 a.m. on the 26th that I knew the left wing of the army was committed to the fight."

I do not know why G.H.Q. Staff did not inform the C.-in-C. sooner. I have described how, about 6·45 a.m., I was sent for by the C.-in-C. to the telephone at Bertry station, and that about 7 a.m. I told the Asst. Chief of the Staff that the Battle had already begun.

Now I was sent for to be told that the C.-in-C. disapproved of my standing to fight, which is clear evidence that he had received the report I sent him in accordance with Field Service Regulations, saying 1 could not carry out his orders to continue retiring.

The following is the note in the 2nd Corps Staff diary on the subject, 2·29 a.m., 26th August:—

*" After consultation with the G.O.C. Cavalry Division and General Officers Commanding Divisions, Commander 2nd Corps decided that retirement in accordance with operation orders was not practicable, but that if any enemy attack in the early morning, it would be necessary to fight on the positions now occupied. G.H.Q. and Divisions informed."*

General Seely too came to me whilst at Bertry station about 7 a.m. having been sent by Sir John French to say he disapproved of my fighting. He probably left G.H.Q. at St. Quentin about 6 a.m.

---

*From an article in the Anglo-French Review for November 1919 by the well-known French Military Historian, General Palat, it is doubtful if any of the B.E.F. should have been east of the forest of Mormal, had General Joffre's instructions been carried out.

Page 83.—Writing of my retirement from Le Cateau, the Field Marshal says: "He was only just in time, for subsequent reports reached me during this motor journey of considerable Uhlan patrols in the neighbourhood, and towards evening St. Quentin itself was threatened by hostile Cavalry, which, however, did not succeed in reaching the town."

Is not this rather a comic argument, and does it not show that the Field Marshal was hard put to it to support his statement that I only just retired in time ?

Surely a few Uhlan patrols, or even a threat of hostile Cavalry, is of itself no real danger to a force such as fought at Le Cateau. That the Uhlans could not have been in force is pretty clear from the evidence of the G.S.O.I. of the Cavalry Division, whose letters I have already quoted. *"From the British Cavalry point of view, I consider that the Huns gave us no trouble at all after Le Cateau, as we were always able to fight delaying actions and retire at our leisure."*

Personally, except for the one moment of doubt already described when I was passing through the village of Maretz about 4 p.m., I was never anxious about my flanks, when once the retirement had begun, for I knew I had retired in time, having ample mounted troops in whom I had every confidence. I imagine the retreat referred to by Lord French must have been on my east or right flank, for there were reports of small patrols of German Cavalry working in that direction, but Allenby's 2½ brigades which were on that flank had no difficulty in keeping them at a distance.

It is possible the Field-Marshal's view was influenced by a discreditable panic which occurred in an ammunition column.

At about 9·30 o'clock that evening when motoring from D'Estreès to St. Quentin, I saw for miles, by the light of my headlamps, boxes of ammunition thrown about on both sides of the road, and I actually found the Commander and the Column just clearing out of St. Quentin *empty*. The O.C. told me some shots had been fired as he came along the road, he believed from Uhlans, and to save his men and horses he had ordered all the ammunition to be thrown away and had galloped away, and seemed very proud of it.

From enquiries I made I came to the conclusion that it was extremely doubtful if there had been any enemy patrols there at all. The Officer was tried by Court-Martial and dismissed the Service, but immediately enlisted, and, I heard, proved himself to be one of our bravest soldiers.

The object of my going to St. Quentin was a two-fold one, first to arrange trains to carry wounded and exhausted men, and secondly to report the situation personally to the C.-in-C. Regarding the first, I found the Director of Railways, Colonel McInnes, in the station and he said the most he could provide was seven trains, and he was doubtful about that, and then only with the Q.M.G.'s consent.

It was about now that I ascertained that the C-in-C. had gone to Noyon, 35 miles further back, G.H.Q. having evacuated St. Quentin and gone there too—information which I submit ought to have been sent me, and probably would have been sent had not an idea prevailed that my force had been surrounded.

Page 84. "Smith-Dorrien reported himself in the early hours of the morning."

*This is quite true.* Knowing how anxious Sir John was, and feeling confident that the good news of the blow we had given the enemy and of our safe retirement must be a relief to him, I motored on with Captain Bowly, my A.D.C., and Prince Henri of Orleans, who was attached to my Headquarters, arriving at Noyon between 12 and 1 on the night 26th-27th, and with some difficulty found G.H.Q. Sir John French and, as far as I recollect, most of the Staff had retired. Shortly however the C.-in-C. appeared, also the Chief of Staff and the Q.M.G. and I explained the situation, expressing myself quite happy about the results of the battle and the safety of the troops.

The C.-in-C. appeared very much worried, and *reproved me before his Staff for being optimistic.* Having made my report, I got permission from the Q.M.G., Sir William Robertson, to obtain any trains Colonel McInnes could give me and I motored back to St. Quentin, arriving there as day was breaking.

On page 85 the Field Marshal tells us of his doings on the 27th August, but to the most important event, so far as the effect on the moral of my Command was concerned, he does not even refer; that was an order which he issued, which came to be referred to for easy recognition as the "sauve qui peut" order.

Unfortunately I have not a copy of the original G.H.Q. order and can only give its reproduction in the orders of the 4th Division:—

*ORDER FROM G.H.Q. ISSUED DURING RETREAT FROM MONS.*

*4th Division.*

*G. 440 twenty-seventh.*

*All ammunition on wagons not absolutely required and other impediments will be off loaded and Officers and men carried to the full capacity of all transport, both horse and mechanical.*

*From—2nd Corps.*
*Place—Ham.*
*Time—10.45 p.m. (27th Aug. 1914).*
*10th Infantry Brigade.*
*11th Infantry Brigade.*
*12th Infantry Brigade.*
*Div. Arty.*
*G.H. 8. Twenty-eighth.*

*All troops will be fed as soon as possible and be ready to move at short notice. All ammunition on wagons not absolutely required and other impediments will be off loaded so that Officers and men can be carried on all transport.*

*From—4th Division.*
*Place—Voyennes.*
*Time—6.55 a.m.*

*Certified true copy,*
*(Sd.) W. G. CHARLES, Capt.,*
*for Lieut.-Col.*
*A.A. & Q.M.G. 4th Division.*

*Reference attached copy of telegram received by 4th Division from 2nd Corps, no copy of the message received from G.H.Q. by 2nd Corps is at present extant in the 2nd Army. The original message appears to have been a telegraphic one, though one report says it was a telephone message. The latter appears unlikely.*

*If a telegram was received it was attached to the War Diary of the 2nd Corps which is now, probably, in London.*

*A copy of the telegram might be in the clearing house of the Signal Service, but would take some time to find.*

*(Sd.) GEO. F. MILNE,*
*M.G.G.S.,*
*29th May, 1915. 2nd Army.*

I will recite how the existence of this Order came to my notice. On the night of the 24th August, 1914, my Headquarters were in Ham, and early next morning, when the Force was again retiring, I met the Brigadier General Commanding the 12th Brigade of the 4th Division, just south of the Somme-Oise Canal. He was on a bicycle having lost his horses; seeing me he dismounted, and remarked that he was afraid my information must be pretty serious, and on my asking why, replied, "Oh, that Order which you've sent out."

I said, "What Order?" and he replied, "The one received early this morning, telling us to lighten our wagons in every possible way so as to get away our men."

I was dumbfounded and said I had never heard of the Order, and further that there was not the smallest necessity for such an order, for the German pursuit was of the feeblest, and was being kept off by the Cavalry and rearguards. The General was immensely relieved and said he was afraid the issue of the Order had already had a demoralising effect, in any case in the 4th Division, where wagons had already been emptied and officers' kits burned.

I naturally went off determined to sift the origin of the Order, but, before doing so, I sent messages to all 3 Divisions, telling them that if they had not already acted on the Order, they were to regard it as cancelled, as the situation throughout my Command was most satisfactory, and the German pursuit feeble and well held.

Fortunately I was in time so far as the 3rd and 5th Divisions were concerned, but too late in the case of the 4th Division. Later on the officers of this Division, whose kits were burnt and had to continue marching and fighting day after day without a change of clothes or boots, were given money compensation on the authority of this order.

None of my staff whom I came across in the next half hour were aware of the Order, but surmised that it had come through as an administrative order during the night, from G.H.Q. and had been sent on to Divisions without reference to me, and this is what really happened.

While I was still much incensed by hearing of this Order, I met the C.-in-C. who had motored up from Noyon, and at once appealed to him, saying that someone had issued this most unnecessary and harmful order, and protested, saying that no reports from me, who was the Commander on the spot, warranted such a serious view being taken as to necessitate such an Order.

I admit I was angry and spoke with some heat, and Sir John retorted that he himself had issued the Order, which in his opinion was quite necessary, and that I again failed to take a serious enough view of the situation.

That the Order had a most depressing effect on the wearied troops there is no doubt.

General Forestier Walker writes as follows of Lord French's book, and I agree with him :—"*There is curiously enough no mention of that order issued to abandon stores, ammunition., &c., an order with regard to which the 2nd Corps Commander made either a written or a personal protest, and which did more to sap the moral of the troops than the retreat itself."*

This was the second time within two days (the first time being at Noyon as already described), that he had taunted me with optimism, and yet pusillanimity and pessimism form a large part of his criticism on me in this book, and perhaps the gravest charge on such counts is the one on page 93 of his book; its inaccuracy is so remarkable that I must deal with it at length.

Writing of events on the 29th August, 1914, and his having consented to carry out the French C.-in-C.'s wish to remain in the line and fill the gap between the 5th and 6th French armies, he states:—" This I had every intention of doing. I am bound to say I had to make this decision in the face of resistance from *some* of my subordinate Commanders, who took a depressed view as to the condition of their troops, When I discussed the situation at a meeting of British Commanders held at Campiègne, Sir Horace Smith-Dorrien expressed it as his opinion that the only course open to us was to retire to our base, thoroughly refit, re-embark, and try to land at some favourable point on the coast line. I refused to listen to what was the equivalent of a Counsel of Despair."

Surely no one could have read so far without coming to the conclusion that in the opinion of the author I, as a General, was worse than useless, in fact a danger to any Force.

I suppose that I should be gratified, since according to the Field Marshal *some* of his subordinate Commanders took a depressed view, to have been singled out as the only one whose actual views are worth quoting, but it would have added interest if he had quoted as well the views of other faint-hearted subordinates.

I should certainly imagine that a plan of action, to have deserved such prominence in history, must have been urged and emphasised with sufficient earnestness to have made some impression on the minds of the other Generals present at the Conference.

Now besides myself there were (I believe) only three other Generals present, namely, Haig, Allenby and Murray—surely he does not suggest that any of those distinguished Generals were for faint-hearted measures and yet they certainly have no recollection of my advocating the pusillanimous line of action Lord French imputes to me; and with their permission I quote from letters from them to me :—

" As regards the question which you ask me, namely, can I remember you saying anything at Campiègne on the 29th

August, 1914, which was of the nature of a Counsel of Despair, or indeed anything which could have been twisted round to such a meaning? I can quite honestly say that I have no recollection of your having done such a thing."

Yours very sincerely,

The Horse Guards,  (Sd.) D. HAIG.
    23rd June, 1919.

---

" I remember the Conference at Campiègne but I have no recollection of your expressing an opinion to the effect that the only course open was to return to the base, re-embark and land elsewhere."

Yours sincerely,

Egypt,  EDMUND H. ALLENBY.
    4th June, 1919.

---

" I have not the least recollection of your urging at Campiègne on the 26th August a return to the Base and re-embarkation. You are perfectly at liberty to make that statement, as also, that I have never known you in the least pessimistic, but on the contrary full of courage at all times."

Ever yours sincerely,<br>(Sd.) ARCHIBALD MURRAY.

Government House,
    Farnborough,
        12th July, 1919.

---

As for myself, beyond denying that I ever gave such counsel, it is unnecessary for me to say more, in view of the opinions of the other three Generals, which I have quoted above.

There is every reason why I should not have given definite advice of any sort, for I really knew very little of the general situation, as may be inferred from many statements in the previous pages, whilst, regarding the local situation, I had every reason to be satisfied, and had on each of the previous two days been reproved for my optimism by the Field Marshal.

Unfortunately the C.-in-C.'s diary for the 29th August, 1914, throws no light on the Conference, in fact it does not even record that a Conference took place—but it had this very illuminating entry:—

"Commander-in-Chief proposed to retire to safe locality in order to refit, which will take eight or ten days. Deficiencies in material very heavy, though Joffre anxious for us to maintain line north of line Campiègne-Soissons. Commander-in-Chief replied impossible."

In the 1st Corps diary of the 29th August there is the following:—

"G.O.C. and S.G.S.O. 1st Corps sent for the G.H.Q. at Campiègne to receive orders for *continued retirement.*"

The 2nd Corps diary of the same date merely records a message saying "C.-in-C. wishes to see General Smith-Dorrien at Campiègne at 3 p.m.

Curiously enough in no diary is the Conference mentioned.

Page 89 "On this day (the 28th August) I inspected a large proportion of the transport of both Army Corps which I found in much better condition than could have been thought possible."

Probably a correct statement, but how much of it would have been in German hands, had we not fought at Le Cateau? (Vide opinion in letter already quoted of G.S.O. of Cavalry Division, Colonel J. Vaughan).

Page 110.—Talking of the decision to advance again, come to on 5th September, he says: "**I despatched Murray at once to visit the Corps and Cavalry Commanders, and ascertain exactly the condition of the troops. He returned later in the day with very favourably reports, all were in excellent spirits and eager for the advance.**"

This may seem an unimportant paragraph to refer to, but to me, if any value is to be given to any of Lord French's statements, it is worth its weight in gold—for has not he said that all were in excellent spirits without excluding the pessimistic and depressed General Smith-Dorrien?

The impression I got from reading the account of the passage of the Marne in "1914" was that it was a great battle for British Arms, whereas the account of the battle of Mons in the same book cannot be recognised as a battle but merely as "an affair."

Now it would be presumption on my part to urge that the strategic conception of the battle of Mons was finer than that of the Marne, but as commander of a corps at both battles I feel I am justified in representing that so far as my corps was concerned the former was a desperate battle reflecting the greatest credit on the dogged bravery of the 2nd Corps, whereas the latter being against flank guards only, was from the fighting point of view comparatively a minor affair.

Although casualties are by no means the only criterion of the strenuousness of a conflict, I submit that they are an indication of some moment.

Now I have already pointed out that the casualties in the 2nd Corps in the two days' fighting at the battle of Mons amounted to over 4,000, and I now quote for comparison the total casualties in the whole of the British Army from the 6th to 10th September, both dates inclusive, and I maintain that the figures are conclusive proof that as a soldier's battle the importance of Mons over the Marne is beyond dispute.

The dates 6th to 10th cover the advance to the Marne, its passage and the end of the battle as fixed by Sir J. French in his despatch of 17th September, 1914, and confirmed by Lord French in his book p. 137.

### APPROXIMATE NUMBER OF CASUALTIES WHICH OCCURRED FROM 6TH TO 10TH SEPTEMBER, 1914,

(Both dates inclusive).

#### REGULAR AND TERRITORIAL FORCES.

|                     | Officers. | Other Ranks. |
|---------------------|-----------|--------------|
| I. Corps            | 45        | 734          |
| II. Corps           | 31        | 623          |
| III. Corps          | 6         | 127          |
| 1st Cavalry Division| 16        | 91           |
| 5th Cavalry Brigade | 5         | 23           |
|                     | 103       | 1,598        |

In describing the Battle of the Marne the Field Marshal certainly does not make out that the 2nd Corps were lacking in push, but on the contrary that they crossed the river before the other Divisions; I feel sure too official history will record that it was certainly not the 2nd Corps which delayed the operation.

Page 128: "His (Smith-Dorrien's) Corps had then (8th September) forced the passage of the river, but had encountered severe opposition in doing so."

On page 133 he says that the 2nd Corps were getting on too fast, and on page 135, talking of the morning of the 10th

September, that he found Smith-Dorrien at Pulteney's Headquarters, and that the 3rd Corps were only then crossing the river.

From my diary of the 9th September (Appendix "A") it will be seen why I was at another Corps Commander's headquarters.

On page 138 Lord French claims that the Germans between the 6th and 12th of September were driven back from the Seine to the Marne, a distance of 65 miles. As a matter of fact the total distance from Melun, his G.H.Q. on the Seine, to Meaux on the Marne, is only 31 miles—and the Germans in front of this, the British Army Section, only came as far south as Coulommier which is less than half way, so they only had some 12 miles to retire to the Marne so far as we were concerned.

On page 154 the Field Marshal talks of visiting all Corps Commanders and finding all confident as to their ability to hold their positions.

I mention this as an instance of my not always appearing to him as pessimistic.

On page 206 he rightly gives high praise to General Pulteney and describes how his (Lord French's) great hope had been to give him Command of an Army. This was in October 1914, and he chose me with Sir Douglas Haig to Command the 1st two Armies in January 1915, and I cannot understand why since he held such a low opinion of me, he missed the opportunity of satisfying his hope.

On pages 209 and 210 the Field Marshal draws attention to the difficult task of the 2nd Corps, fighting in the low lying water-logged and enclosed ground between Bethune and La Bassée, and to the north of that line. He certainly does not minimise the task, but why should he go out of his way to make a statement which can only lower me in the minds of readers who are not acquainted with the Field Marshal's style? The statement reads:—

"On the afternoon of the 14th October, I again visited Smith-Dorrien at Bethune—he was in one of those fits of deep depression which unfortunately visited him frequently. He complained that the 2nd Corps had never got over what he described as the shock of Le Cateau and that the officers sent out to him to replace his tremendous losses in the officers, were untrained and inexperienced, and lastly he expressed himself convinced that there was no great fighting spirit throughout the troops he commanded," and a few lines further on the Field Marshal softens the previous unpleasant remarks by saying: "**Even if, as I consider, his point of view was needlessly pessimistic, Smith-Dorrien was certainly confronted with a difficult task**" for which remark I am grateful.

All who knew me and worked with me in France will scorn the accusation that I was given to fits of pessimistic depression and so I will not argue that point—but I cannot accept the statement that I said the troops had no great fighting spirit, for they were fighting grandly—I forget exactly what I said, but I have no doubt I emphasised strongly that my ranks were depleted by heavy losses, and that, good as my new material might be, loss of highly trained officers and non-commissioned officers was telling in the difficult task before us—and I maintain that I was right to acquaint the C.-in-C. with the true state of affairs—as it was essential that he should appreciate what the real situation was. I have no doubt I was not very cheerful that day—I had that morning lost my old friend and great stand-by General Hubert Hamilton, the Commander of the 3rd Division and my diary app. "A" for 14th October will give some idea of how deeply I felt it. On the two previous days, the 12th and 13th, I had had a thousand casualties in the two divisions—I was on a front of 8 miles with no reserves—my ranks were attenuated, some of the battalions being only about ½ strength—my left flank was *en l'air*, except for some French Cavalry, who were not under my orders and of whose movements I had no certain knowledge.

That I did not overestimate the task before me is proved by the fact that in the 20 days from 12th to 31st October, the total casualties in my Corps of two *weak* Divisions amounted to 375 officers and 9,184 other ranks—*total 9559*.

My losses then (*i.e.*, up to 11th October) since the opening of the campaign, about 7 weeks, amounted to about 12,500.

I have received the following uninvited criticism on the Field Marshal's ungenerous insinuation from Major-General Sir G. Forestier Walker:—

"**Page 210—On the afternoon of the 14th I again visited Smith-Dorrien at Bethune** ..............."

"*General Smith-Dorrien's headquarters were not at Bethune, though the C.-in-C. might have met him there. As I was not present I cannot say what occurred, but I, who must have seen more of the General at that time than anyone else, and have had far better opportunities of seeing him in such moods, if he did indulge in them, do most emphatically assert that, from first to last of my intimate relationship with him, I never saw him in a mood which could possibly be described as one of deep depression.*

*Things were often enough pretty desperate in those days which were the worst I have experienced in this war, but Sir Horace was throughout wonderful in concealing the anxiety which at times it was impossible that he could not but feel, and I owe much to him for his example in this particular."*

Pages 221 & 222—" Orders were sent to Rawlinson to move on and attack that place on the 18th—he did not march," later he remarks "I do not impute blame for this to the Commander of the 4th Corps. Such instances of disregard of orders occur in every campaign. Only when the full history of the war is known and all the cards are laid on the table, can a right judgment be formed."

That he was right not to blame Rawlinson, I feel sure, and merely quote the incident to show that the Field-Marshal is quite ready to forgive in one Corps Commander what he condemns in me, and this, so far as I am concerned, after studying only a table on which some of the most important cards came from the wrong pack.

Page 223.—Lord French having praised the splendid advances of the 3rd Corps, considers that the 2nd Corps might have made further progress between 12th and 15th October, had it been directed with more determination and vigour. I merely regard this as an opinion of recent birth to help to bolster up his contention that it was because he had an incompetent and feeble General in Command of the 2nd Corps, that he had to continue retiring in August, in spite of the protest of the Home Government and our Allies.

The quotation (p. 224) in support of his views, of a wireless from a German General is probably as worthless as the one he gave describing how few troops there were opposite the British at Le Cateau, which Von Kluck has now shown to be entirely misleading.

Lord French knows perfectly well that bogus wireless telegrams are part of the game of war.

Page 239.—In his description of the splendid valour of the troops at the first Battle of Ypres, it comes as balm to the feelings of the 2nd Corps which are so accustomed to being wounded in this book, to read the following:—

" It was only a slightly less arduous task which fell upon the 2nd Corps in this great Battle, for they had a long line to hold in a much more difficult country and were subjected to powerful attacks by superior numbers. There is indeed little distinction to be made between the troops who fought so bravely all along the line, all were doggedly tenacious and all were superhumanly brave—the fullest measure of mutual support was assured by the complete understanding and perfect loyalty which existed amongst leaders of all ranks, combined with the alertness shown by all Commanders in filling up gaps in the line without delay, &c., &c."

This is high praise, and unless the paragraph be corrected in a later edition, General Smith-Dorrien is included in it.

Page 240.—Talking of events about the 2nd November the Field Marshal says: "the condition of the 2nd Corps was again causing me anxiety, and the Corps Commander was calling out for help and reinforcements."

All perfectly true. My casualties from 12th October to 3rd November amounted to 10,883, and my battalions were mere skeletons, so that my request for reinforcements was natural and proper, a fact which would hardly be inferred from the Field Marshal's method of expression.

Page 337.—Lord French writes of the 23rd December:— "On my return to Headquarters I met Haig and Smith-Dorrien who had come to lunch, and I discussed with them my wish to form " armies " immediately. I wished Haig to command the 1st, 4th and Indian Corps as the 1st Army, and Smith-Dorrien the 2nd, 3rd and the 5th Corps as the 2nd Army. Orders to this effect came out on Christmas night."

I think all who have read the pages of "1914" will be astounded that out of all his Generals, Sir John French should have selected one, who, if what he has said of him in the pages of his book is worthy of credence, was unfit to command an Army Corps.

This is the last criticism I have to offer on the Field Marshal's book, in so far as his remarks depreciate the work of the 2nd Corps, and are inaccurate as regards myself.

The facts and figures on which I rely are borne out by all contemporary evidence and official records, and I am content to leave the decision as to the justice or otherwise of his strictures and suggestions to the verdict of any impartial reader.

# APPENDIX A.

### EXTRACT FROM GENERAL SIR H. SMITH-DORRIEN'S DIARY, 1914.

N.B.—In the copies of the diary sent to the King many names of both places and people were left blank.

---

21st August.—Arrived at Amiens, and directed by General Robb to Le Cateau, and eventually to Landrecies, where I arrived about 3 p.m. I motored from there to the Headquarters of my Army Corps at Bavai; having discussed the situation with my Staff there and ascertained that Haig's Corps was moving on my right, I motored into Le Cateau and saw the Commander-in-Chief. Starting back at about 9 p.m., I found the road blocked and firing going on between French territorial troops and our own, under a misapprehension, unfortunately one of our men was killed and two wounded. I got back to my Headquarters about 11 p.m. and issued orders to continue our move North to-morrow.

22nd August.—As news of the German advances West and South of Brussels created an interesting situation, we had a very interesting day pushing forward to the line of the Canal in the neighbourhood of Mons, where I was ordered to watch with my Corps along the Canal. Haig's Corps was slightly thrown back on our right. Our Cavalry Division, as well as the 5th Division, were engaged all day in the neighbourhood of Binche, and achieved undoubted success, Captain Hornby, of the 4th Dragoon Guards, distinguishing himself by charging and routing with his Squadron a small body of Cavalry, and bringing back some prisoners. It was evident from the news that large forces of the enemy were approaching us, and that a fight to-morrow was a certainty. The French are in line on our immediate right, past Charleroi, almost to Namur. We have been pushed forward before we have really completed our mobilization (for sundry units have not yet joined, especially some of the Field Hospitals and Artillery) at the urgent request of the French, so as to be in a position to cover their left flank, which we are to do at once. The Mons salient, which is held by the 8th Brigade, is almost an impossible one to defend, but I gather it is not expected that this is to be treated as a defensive position.

23rd August, Sunday.—Outposts attacked early all along the line, at first not in great forces, but increasing steadily all day. I went out to the outposts in a motor, and in going along them a shell just missed the car. The Germans apparently were firing high explosives of a very virulent nature. In order to cover a certain withdrawal from the untenable salient at Mons, I had had an entrenchment made in rear of it to prevent the enemy debouching to the South. Some desperate fighting took place in this neighbourhood. The Royal Fusiliers, who were at the very point, suffering considerably, but were withdrawn through the town of Mons by the help of the Middlesex and Royal Irish on their right flank, but both these regiments lost heavily. It is reported that the Middlesex have lost half their strength. At this period, the 5th Division, which was on my left, was not so heavily attacked, but in the afternoon the enemy's Infantry worked forward across the Canal, although we had blown up a good many of the bridges, and about 7 p.m. I heard they had penetrated our line in the neighbourhood of Frameries. Directly I heard this information, as I had not a single man to put in to support my left, I motored straight to Haig's Headquarters, about four miles off, and asked for the help of the 5th Infantry Brigade, which was within 5,000 yards of the point where the Germans were penetrating my line. This he readily gave, and they got up so quickly that the Germans were forced back and the whole line was cleared again. This was how matters stood about two hours after dark. During the night, there was some very heavy street fighting in the neighbourhood of Frameries. The whole of the position we were occupying, especially from Frameries, Westward from the 5th Division portion, is a series of mines and miners' houses, very broken country indeed, and very difficult to fight in. However, I was quite happy after the result of the day's fight, and from what I heard of the men's spirits and from the number of Germans who had been killed, and that we had held our own well so long as our flanks were not turned. It was during the afternoon, when the fight was going on, that Allenby's Cavalry Division had been moved across our rear to our left flank, in the neighbourhood of Thulin, a very difficult operation requiring excellent staff work, and it was most successfully accomplished.

24th August.—At about 3 a.m., I received an Order from Headquarters that, in consequence of the French on our right having fallen back instead of advancing, both our flanks were exposed, and that, as several German Army Corps were engaged against us, it would be necessary to retire. Of course, before we could do so, all our baggage and impedimenta had to be cleared away. I saw Haig, and we settled on a course of action, as we both fully realised that we were in for a very heavy day's fighting and that the operation of withdrawal in the face of such numbers was a very serious and difficult one. Dawn saw the enemy commencing a vigorous attack, and owing to a gap in the line caused by the removal of two battalions on the right of the 5th Division—a very excusable accident considering the nature of the country—the 5th Division had to fight a very severe action, although perhaps not more severe, at any rate at first, than the action of the 3rd Division retiring from before Mons. All day the fight continued, whilst we were gradually falling back. Some very fine deeds were performed this day. At one time, in order to save the 5th (Fergusson's) Division's left flank, the 2nd Cavalry Brigade under De Lisle executed a most gallant but not very effective charge against a large force, estimated at a Division of the German Infantry and guns in action in that neighbourhood. The Cavalry Brigade lost heavily, though not so heavily as we thought at first, for a good many of them got away afterwards and rejoined. Nightfall saw us (the B.E.F.) on the line Maubeuge-Bavai-Wargnies, the men tired, hungry, but extremely cheerful, and they all felt that they had done well, which no doubt they had. Bavai was the dividing point between the two Army Corps.

25th August.—Moving all impedimenta off 2 a.m., the retirement was ordered to a line running about East and West through Le Cateau, a very long march considering the state of the troops of over 20 miles, and in many cases 30. It will be noticed from the map that what makes the operation a still more difficult and complicated one is the fact that we are not retiring moving straight to our rear, but diagonally away to the West, thus making our West flank very much more difficult to cover, as well as complicating the movement of our impedimenta. A lot of fighting took place this day, and Haig's Army—in some way of which I have no knowledge—instead of coming back into line with my own, kept much further East and North and halted, leaving a gap of some ten miles between us. The 4th Division (General Snow), fresh from England, had taken up a position to the West of Le Cateau to help the retirement which it did most nobly—remaining out and allowing our tired rearguards to come through, and acting as a pivot for our Cavalry to fall back on, and indeed in some cases behind. It was very difficult to realise the situation of all one's troops, and it was not until about 1·30 a.m. on the 26th that I fully realised the state of affairs, which was that the troops in this theatre of operations consisted of the whole of the Cavalry Division under Allenby, the 4th Division under Snow, and the 19th Brigade under Drummond (who had gone sick), besides my own Corps, consisting of the 3rd and 5th Divisions. Haig, I know, was fighting a long way off, and also that there were columns of Germans between us, in addition to those following round our West flank.

26th August.—I had received distinct orders to continue the retirement at dawn. The position of all the troops in this area was very scattered, the men were very tired, there was a very large force of the enemy in close touch with us all along the line, and a very good chance of the retirement developing into a rout. I therefore decided to assume command of all the troops, and I told General Allenby and General Snow that the Cavalry and 4th Divisions respectively would come under my command, and that I had decided to send all our baggage away at once in the direction of the line Beaurevoir-Le Catelets. I had received orders yesterday generally as to the position to be taken up, some of which had already been lightly entrenched. The line generally was from the South side of Le Cateau through the villages of Troisvilles-Audencourt-Caudry, with the left thrown back on Hautcourt; the 5th Division on the right, 3rd Division in centre, and 4th Division on left. The Cavalry Division which was tremendously scattered early that morning—2½ Brigades being at Catillon, East of Le Cateau, and 1¾ Brigades near Caudry\*. I arranged with General Allenby that the Caudry\* lot should fall back on Ligny and try and guard my left flank, and the others from Catillon should guard my right flank. The French Cavalry Corps, under General Sordet, which had moved across South of us from East to West the previous day, promised to help us in the neighbourhood of Cambrai. The situation was not a pleasing one. Soon after dawn, the enemy commenced their attack, which increased in intensity all the morning. At about 7 a.m., I, from Bertry, where my Headquarters were throughout the battle, got through on the telephone to General H. Wilson at St. Quentin. I explained the state of affairs, and that we should put up a real grand fight, but that as our men were too weary to march there was a possibility, with both our flanks *en l'air* and a vastly superior number of the enemy against us, of our being surrounded. I strongly deprecated Sir John French's coming to us, as he wished to, explaining that it was essential for the good of the cause for which we were fighting that he should be free to go to England, if I was unable to extricate the Force. The enemy's gun fire was tremendous, and this was accounted for after-

---
\*This evidently should be Vièsly.

wards, as there were $3\frac{1}{2}$ Corps against $1\frac{1}{2}$. Subsequently, our Army Headquarters estimated, there was the Artillery of 5 Army Corps in action against us. It is impossible to describe briefly the incidents of the day's fighting. At one time the left flank, the 4th Division, was forced back, but later on regained their ground. The villages of Caudry, Audencourt and Troisville were the scenes of very heavy fighting, and many acts of bravery, and later, when the line fell back, Ligny was the scene of desperate fighting. The 5th Division on the right was very much exposed, and the shell fire which they had to put up with for seven or eight hours was very demoralising, and at 2·30 General Fergusson sent to me to say he feared the troops could stand it no longer and were beginning to dribble away. I then issued instructions to the rest of the troops what to do in case they fell back. It was unfortunate, as everywhere else the troops were holding their own well, and in fact were driving the Germans back. All I had under my own hands as a Reserve were two Battalions and a Battery, and these I had already made use of once, but I sent them off again to take up a position to cover the retirement of the 5th Division. About 3 o'clock the retirement commenced. The 5th Division were in great disorder, and retreated along the straight Roman road via Maretz-Preamont-Estrees. The 3rd Division and the 4th Division retired more regularly, and the French Cavalry did real good work in protecting our exposed or West flank. I forgot to say that a considerable force of Germans had turned the right flank, and it was at that point that the shell fire had forced the 5th Division to retire. To make matters worse, it came on a very heavy rain, and it was a sorry crowd that worked their way back into St. Quentin that night. There was practically no attempt at pursuit, except with the gun fire. At 9 p.m., I left to see Sir John French at St. Quentin, and found he had already gone on 35 miles further to Noyon. Having arranged at St. Quentin for some trains to pick up weary troops, I went on and saw Sir John, and I got back to my force again as dawn was breaking at St. Quentin.

27th August.—My troops were very much scattered, but still not as badly as they had been at Le Cateau the day before. Divisional Commanders had done extremely well, and also Brigadiers. There was nothing for it except further retirement. Some of the troops yesterday, after fighting all day, had marched back for 25 miles. Great efforts were made by the Staff to get units together as much as possible, but as some of them had lost almost all their officers it was not for the next two or three days that we were able to get certain of them together, but taking it altogether the retirement was a very orderly one, and we fell back during this day about 15 miles South of the Somme River, and Canal on the line Nesle-Ham-Flavy. The rearguard had a good deal of fighting, but were never seriously pressed. It was during this day I regret to say Colonel Boileau, the C.S.O. of the 3rd Division, was very dangerously wounded. Throughout the day, I had very alarming reports of rearguards *in extremis* having thrown in their last reserves, but all of them proved to be untrue. I am afraid a good number of our best officers have been killed or wounded, but it is impossible in the scattered state of units, with so many of their staff, clerks, &c., killed or missing, to make out any accurate returns. A lot of men are sure to appear again, as they lost their way in the night retirement and wandered into other Columns, but at present the 3rd Division alone considers their casualties amount to 150 officers and over 5,000 other ranks, but these I am sure will be very largely reduced. The effect of the enemy's shell fire is very trying to nerves, and there are few who were under it who are not more or less shaken. *During the night, a most alarming order from General Headquarters was received that we must continue the retirement at once, lightening our wagons by throwing away ammunition, &c., to carry weary men. I am at a loss to know why this order has been issued, and conclude the Headquarters know something we do not. I am afraid the order has had a bad effect on some of the officers and men, whose nerves have been shattered by the heavy fighting and want of sleep.*

28th August.—Again off in the middle of the night to the line of the Oise about Noyon. I was able this day to see a lot of the troops on the march, and talk to them, and tell them that the true reason for retirement was not that we had been beaten, but that it was part of the French strategical plan to go on falling back to draw the enemy further from their own base. I was particularly struck by the splendid march discipline of the Artillery—the 15th Brigade had lost all its guns except two, and they made a brave show as they marched along the roads. The 3rd and 4th Divisions during this day were unable to reach the Oise, having been bothered a good deal by the enemy's Horse Artillery and Cavalry. The men are all desperately tired, and I am not surprised. Some of the Staffs of Brigades and Divisions are quite worn out, and almost unequal to working out Orders. My own Staff are all very tired, but are doing splendidly. I reckon that I myself have not averaged two hours sleep during the last six days. My Headquarters to-night are in a beautiful Chateau in the village of **Cuts.**

29th August.—Had quite a good sleep of four hours. My efforts were first directed at withdrawing the 3rd and 4th Divisions across the Oise. The Cavalry were all very busily engaged with detachments of the enemy, and large columns were seen by aeroplanes some miles away moving down on us. About 11 a.m. De Lisle's (2nd) Cavalry Brigade was attacked in the neighbourhood of Plessis, between Ham and Guiscard, and did extremely well, but I had to send forward two Brigades, one from each of the 3rd and 4th Divisions, to his support. De Lisle had a certain number of casualties, Lieutenant Sanderson, 4th Dragoon Guards, being killed. That evening, I received Orders to continue the withdrawal South, and I moved my Headquarters before dark to a farm some five miles further South. There was a very dense fog in the early morning, ending in great heat. General Pulteney and his Staff arrived to take command of the 3rd Army Corps, which only consisted of the 4th Division and 19th Infantry Brigade. These troops I am to hand over to him to-morrow. During this day, an attack of the 18th, 3rd, 10th and 1st French Corps in the direction of St. Quentin was supposed to have been successful. I was sent for by Sir John French in Compeigne, and found General Joffre there, also Generals Allenby and Haig. Joffre was under the impression that his attack that day had been successful and it was not until afterwards that we heard it had failed.

4th September.—I met Sir John French at Haig's Headquarters at 3·30 p.m., and we discussed the whole plan of campaign. It is very pleasing to me to hear again from the Commander-in-Chief praise of the way I had extricated my Force, and also of the injury I had inflicted on the enemy by deciding to fight the battle at Le Cateau on the 26th August; Sir John also expressed to me over and over again his absolute confidence in me, which was decidedly pleasing to hear.

6th September.—Sir John French came to see me, and was most complimentary, repeating what he had said to me before, that our determined action in fighting the Battle of Le Cateau had saved the whole situation, and that he was referring to it in such terms in his despatch.

9th September.—The 3rd Corps, Pulteney's, which had to cross at La Ferte, found the bridges blown up and the far side strongly held by Artillery, Infantry and Machine guns. It was this that exposed the left flank of Fergusson's Division, for the ground between that and La Ferte is high, and gave good positions to the enemy. About 11·30, I went to

Pulteney's headquarters to see if I could help him in any way by pushing in between Fergusson and himself, but he seemed to think that he would be able to manage it. Whilst talking to him, Sir John French arrived, and expressed himself very pleased with the way my Corps was pushing on. He told me that the 1st Corps, which ought to be in line with us, was somewhere behind.

14th October, Wednesday.—A very wet morning, and a good deal of Artillery—mostly on our side.

This to me is the saddest day of the Campaign, for Hubert Hamilton was killed by a chance shell. He was standing with some of his Staff and a shrapnel burst near him, and one bullet struck him on the temple and killed him instantaneously. Not only do I lose a very old friend but a most exceptional Commander, and one who inspired all under him with absolute confidence.

I visited General Fergusson in the course of the morning. His troops are well entrenched, but are under considerable shell fire—though I do not think as heavy as the Germans are under, for we appear to have more guns in action, and are not sparing ammunition.

At 2 p.m., I met the C.-in-C. by appointment in Bethune, and we discussed the whole situation. He is very pleased with the work of our Cavalry Corps, and Gough, as usual, appears to have distinguished himself in capturing a most important tactical point at Mont Noir, in a range of hills some 17 miles North-West of Lille. Pulteney's 3rd Corps, too, has made some progress, but had a good deal of fighting yesterday. There is, however, a wide gap—of eight miles at least—between his Corps and mine, and a good many German troops in it.

In the afternoon, I went to call on General Maistre, commanding the XXI. French Corps—the Corps on my right, with whom I am co-operating—but unfortunately he had gone forward to some Village, and later in the evening he came to see me. He seems a very agreeable person, and I think very capable.

Owing to the shell fire, it was not possible to bury poor Hamilton until after dark. I shall never forget the scene. It took place in the churchyard of the Village of Lacouture, about a mile from where he had fallen. The Church itself was only about half a mile behind our firing line. It was a very dark night, and at about 8.30 as many officers as could be collected from the fighting line, all his Staff and several of mine assembled and marched in procession into the churchyard. All the time a determined night attack was being made by the Germans all along our line and just in front of the Church was very heavy indeed, so much so that the rattle of machine guns, musketry and artillery fire made it very difficult to hear the Chaplain, the Revd. Macpherson, read the Service. Quite unmoved by the heavy fire, much of it over our heads at the time, the Chaplain read the funeral service beautifully. It was quite the most impressive funeral I have ever seen or am ever likely to see—and quite the most appropriate to the gallant soldier and fine leader we were laying in his last resting place. I fancy all were much moved by the scene—as I was myself.

Our casualties to-day were quite considerable.

## APPENDIX B.

The following appeared in the *Weekly Dispatch* of the 18th February, 1917.—It is the only account of any part I took in the war, which has been published *as coming from me*.

I have explained in the body of my statement how it came to be written.

Composed as it was by the Editor, from a brief conversation on the Telephone I regard it as, although inaccurate in detail on the whole, a remarkably graphic and correct account. The only passage I can cavil at is the one giving my reasons for being unable to carry out my orders to retire, for the most compelling reasons do not appear :—

### 'HOW THE OLD BRITISH ARMY DIED.'

GENERAL SIR HORACE SMITH-DORRIEN INTERVIEWED ON THE HISTORIC RETREAT FROM MONS.

Now that the old British Army which fought at Mons is but a glorious memory, never to be forgotten, and we are about to witness, I hope, the final triumph of the millions who have taken its place, perhaps one who had the honour to command a part of the original Expeditionary Force may be permitted to pay a slight tribute to the valour and resource of the men who did so much to stem the tide of the German flood into France.

I do not know how many are left of that little Army. Their numbers must be very few. Some of the men of Mons are in the trenches to-day; but they have become merged in the new armies, and I sincerely hope that they will survive to see the complete overthrow of the enemy, who came so near to exterminating the little force that barred their path in August 1914.

I do not suppose that any Army in the world has ever had a more highly trained, a better disciplined force than that which took up its positions at Mons. The difference between the old Army and the new was that which really tells—years of steady training, both in musketry and in field operations.

What really stopped the Germans at Mons was the extraordinarily accurate fire of our infantry, which mowed down the enemy in large numbers.

The new Army has been trained in a very short space of time and everything has been concentrated in getting them ready to hold their own in trench warfare, and it is not very probable that they would have been very successful had they been called upon to perform the operation that was imposed on the Expeditionary Force.

\* \* \*

The explanation is this: There is a great disparity between the time necessary for training men for open field operations and the time required for a few definite movements, such as holding trenches and making attacks from them. For one thing, it is doubtful whether the newly trained men could keep up the same accuracy of rifle fire and have the same confidence in their rifles. Yet there is no question that they have proved themselves superior to the new German levies and that they will be equal to any demands that may be made upon them in the future.

In conversation one man recently said to me:

"But, after all, the old British Army did not really stop the Germans—did they?"

I had to assure him that they did stop the Germans, although the odds were about four to one and although subsequently at Ypres they were painfully short of guns and ammunition.

Consider the situation as it appeared to the British Command shortly after the Army had disembarked and was moving forward to meet the Germans. From information received by our Headquarters from the French, we believed that one, and certainly not more than two, enemy army corps were advancing to the attack—100,000 men at the most and about 350 guns. Against these we had 80,000 men and 280 guns, so that we felt quite competent to hold our own. No thought of retreat was in our minds. We were to begin an offensive and made our plans accordingly.

My line was along the canal between Condé and Mons, on the extreme left, and Sir Douglas Haig's corps was on my right, stretching from Mons to Binche.\*

\* \* \* \*

Along this front was the flower of the British Army—most of the famous regiments, whose names had become a tradition through the centuries of England's wars. With me were the Bedfords, the Cornwalls, the Cheshires, Duke of Wellington's,

---

\*Evidently a very approximate description.

the Dorsets, the East Surreys, the Gordons, the King's Own Scottish Borderers, the Lincolns, the Manchesters, the Middlesex, the Norfolks, the Northumberland Fusiliers, the Royal Fusiliers, the Royal Irish, the Royal Irish Rifles, the Royal Scots, the Royal Scots Fusiliers, the South Lancashires, the Suffolks, the West Kents, the Worcesters, the Wiltshires, and the Yorkshire Light Infantry.

These were among the men who went to meet the first onslaught of the greatest Continental army that had ever taken the field. They had come across the Channel singing popular airs and imbued with the most wonderful spirit of cheerfulness and confidence ever witnessed in any body of soldiers.

The first fighting began on Sunday, August 23, with outpost affairs at first, and by noon the armies were getting to closer grips. It early became manifest that the enemy were in much stronger force than we had believed. Their artillery was very powerful, and they certainly had many more guns than 350, but so early in the action it was not possible to form a really reliable estimate.

The fighting continued all day and through the night.

At one point of the canal there was a dangerous salient which would obviously be the objective of a heavy attack, so a second line of defence was prepared so that when, as was to be expected, the men holding the salient had to give way they should be able to fall back and take up new positions. This new line ran from a bridge over the canal, west of Mons, along a road toward the south-east.

\* \* \* \*

The retirement at this point was successfully performed and we were holding our new position with confidence until at 3 a.m. on the 24th orders reached me that the Army was to retire. Up to that time all our preparations were still for an offensive. Our ammunition columns and field ambulances were all close up to the lines ready for a forward move.

This meant that the roads along which we were to make our retirement were encumbered with an enormous amount of heavy traffic, and all of it had to be cleared away before the Army could make a steady and properly organised movement to the rear.

For such a sudden change of plans time was the all-important factor. If only the news had reached us earlier the work of clearing the roads behind might have been done during the night. As it happened, by the time we got all this impedimenta out of the way and were able to withdraw our fighting troops it was 9 or 10 o'clock.

It appears that disquieting news had reached the Commander-in-Chief, and the despatch which Sir John French wrote subsequently explains this. It reads as follows:

"In the meantime, about 5 p.m., I received a most unexpected message from General Joffre by telegraph telling me that at least three German corps—viz., a reserve corps, the 4th Corps, and the 9th Corps—were moving on my position in front, and that the 2nd Corps was engaged in a turning movement from the direction of Tournay. He also informed me that the two reserve French Divisions and the 5th French Army on my right were retiring, the Germans having on the previous day gained possession of the passages of the Sambre between Charleroi and Namur.

"In view of the possibility of my being driven from the Mons position I had previously ordered a position in rear to be reconnoitred. This position rested on the fortress of Maubeuge on the right and extended west to Jenlain, south-east of Valenciennes, on the left. The position was reported difficult to hold because standing crops and buildings made the siting of trenches very difficult and limited the field of fire in many important localities. It nevertheless afforded a few good artillery positions.

"When the news of the retirement of the French and the heavy German threatening on my front reached me I endeavoured to confirm it by aeroplane reconnaissance; and as a result of this I determined to effect a retirement to the Maubeuge position at daybreak on the 24th."

\* \* \* \*

It was a very long retirement—a distance of 25 miles to the position of Le Cateau. The 1st Corps had halted at Landrecies, some eight miles short of this position.

I managed to get into touch with the 4th Division, the 19th\* Brigade, and the Cavalry Division, none of which were under my orders, and I gave them my plan of battle and told them what positions to take up and that I had decided to make a strong stand there. I issued orders describing what roads were to be taken if in the course of the battle it was necessary to retire. Thus all knew what was expected of them.

Meanwhile I had received orders from Sir John French not to make a stand at Le Cateau but to continue retiring. These orders I could not see my way to obey, for I feared, with the men tired as they were, further retirement might end in a rout, and also I considered that to show our teeth was the only way of stopping the enemy.

---

\*The 19th Bde. was put under orders of 2nd Corps on afternoon of 25th but were taken away again the same evening. The 4th Division was not placed under the 2nd Corps.

I therefore informed the Commander-in-Chief by telephone of my decision. I said that before I could retire I must fight and that in order to avoid a disaster a hard blow must be dealt the Germans.

In reply I was informed that I was risking a Sedan. I said that I was prepared to take that risk, and it was suggested to me that Sir John might be willing to come and take over the command. But I was anxious not to avoid the responsibility. I thought if there was going to be a Sedan that, for the sake of the cause of the Allies, Sir John should be able to return to England and organise a new Army.

Personally I had fears that there might be a Sedan, but I could not see what other course I could take to save my force.

\* \* \* \*

At 7 a.m. on August 26 the Germans had a tremendous circle of guns extending right along our whole front, and the battle began. My only hope was to hold on until nightfall. But I never expected to do so, because we had had no time to construct trenches of any value. The ground was very open and both of my flanks were in the air.

A cavalry corps under General Sordet which had been at Charleroi on the 25th had passed through my lines going east to west on my left flank.

I did not meet General Sordet, but I sent an urgent message to him saying that I was going to fight and that I hoped he would be able to cover my left. I got back no reply, but at about 4 p.m., when our retirement had commenced, I heard the sound of heavy firing beyond the left flank, and I feared that the Germans had got round and were coming towards my rear. I rode off in this direction with an aide-de-camp to learn it was not the Germans but Sordet's gallant cavalry who were beating off the enemy.

The French cavalry rendered magnificent service on this day, and I felt that I must pay a tribute to their timely intervention, so I sent a message of cordial thanks to the commander.

On my right wing there was a gap of eight miles, with nobody between my corps and the left of the 1st corps. I asked the Cavalry Division commanded by General Allenby to watch that flank, and this was very well done by the 1st Cavalry Brigade.

\* \* \* \*

In spite of these safeguards, however, between one and two o'clock the reports came that the 5th Division were getting very badly pummelled and were being knocked to pieces by the German artillery. On the right flank there was at least a division of the enemy infantry, and a report reached me that the men could not hold out any longer, but were beginning to dribble away. Some 40 out of the 70 guns of this division had been knocked out.

On receipt of this news I sent an order for the 5th Division to retire and for the other divisions, the 3rd and 4th, to conform.

Between 2·30 and 3 p.m. the 5th Division was on the move. A great number of battalions, through loss of officers and non-commissioned officers, were in a great state of disorder, but there was never any suggestion of panic. The men were as calm as possible, smoking their pipes and streaming away like a crowd from the Derby and covered by two battalions of the 19th Brigade and a battery which had been kept as a reserve, and they did their work admirably.

In Sir Henry Newbolt's "Tales of the Great War" there is the best and most accurate account I have read of this retirement—although I do not agree with much of the praise that the author gives me for the part that I played. He quotes this account by Lieutenant Longman, of the 4th Royal Fusiliers, one of General Hamilton's reserve battalions:

"At 1 p.m., a lull—we all thought we had beaten them off. Suddenly a tremendous burst of firing in the centre of our line; 3·30, order for a general retirement. Then I saw a sight I hope never to see again. Our line of retreat was down two roads, which converged on a village about a mile behind the position.

\*     \*     \*     \*

"Down these roads came a mob—men from any regiment there, guns, riderless horses, limbers packed with wounded, quite unattended and lying on each other, jostling over ruts, etc.

"It was not a rout, only complete confusion. This was the Germans' chance. One battery of artillery sent forward, or one squadron of cavalry, would have turned this rabble into a complete rout and the whole Army would have been cut up piece-meal.

"Meanwhile we were the only regiment I saw in any order. We had not been engaged, and had only lost one officer and about 30 men; we had also had a hot meal, so that we were in good condition. We went back in a succession of extended lines, in absolute order, and formed up behind a farmhouse near where the roads met.

"Here we waited in mass while the rest of the Army streamed past. It was a most trying half-hour. It seemed inevitable that they would follow up, and then the jam in the village would have been indescribable—I have since heard that they had sustained fearful losses, and also a division of French cavalry was covering our retreat.

"When the rabble had got past we moved off, marching at attention, arms sloped, fours dressed, etc., through the village; 7 p.m., moved off again and marched till 1 a.m."

The other two divisions, who had been in very heavy fighting all day, disliked very much receiving the order to retire, as they felt that they were holding their own and at any rate giving the enemy as much as they got, but, of course, they obeyed the order. Their retirement, performed as an operation of war, was as perfect as could possibly be imagined. There was no disorder, no lack of discipline, everything working like a machine.

\* \* \* \*

At about four o'clock in the afternoon it had come on very wet after the intense heat. By seven o'clock we had gone altogether some 9 or 10 miles. It was dark, and we halted for a few hours, and so the men got a little of the rest they were so greatly in need of.

Owing to the very heavy punishment the enemy had received they were unable to harass us, and the spirit of our men was perfectly splendid. I shall never forget the marvellous cheerfulness of every one of them. They did not look like a defeated army, as indeed they were not. The casualties had, of course, been pretty heavy, and some of the men were very tired, but one could hardly expect anything else considering that a very large percentage of the men in each of the battalions were Reservists, only called up on mobilisation, and had not previous to that been doing any marching or physical exercise. And yet they had endured over eighty hours of marching and fighting.

For the next ten days the retirement continued, and I am sure that the men did not realise why it was necessary, although we did our best to explain the situation to them.

On September 6 the joyful news came that we were again to advance, and it is impossible to describe the extraordinary effect it had upon all the troops. There was a smile on every face as the men went forward, driving the enemy before them until the line of the Aisne was reached, where the enemy had taken up an impregnable position. Then trench warfare commenced until the first week in October, when the British Army was relieved on the Aisne by French troops and moved north into Flanders, again having open fighting until the first battle of Ypres.

From this time the war movement ceased and the long-drawn-out trench warfare began.

The principal task of the old British Army had been performed. Together with their gallant French Allies they destroyed the German ambition of conquest, and in that first month they sealed the doom of the Empire which thought to override all Europe and the world.

xviii.

# APPENDIX C.

Specimen of the class of article which appeared, and remaining uncontradicted, gave an entirely misleading impression of Le Cateau to the public.

If the facts had been as given in this article many of the criticisms would have been deserved. There can be no doubt that Mr. Lovat Fraser honestly believed the story of the battle as described by him to be the correct one.

---

### SHOULD GENERAL SMITH-DORRIEN HAVE DISOBEYED LORD FRENCH'S ORDERS?

#### A criticism of Sir Horace's story of Le Cateau, by LOVAT FRASER.

In *The Weekly Dispatch* last Sunday, General Sir Horace Smith-Dorrien gave in an interview his version of the retreat from Mons, and explained his reasons for fighting the battle of Le Cateau on August 26, 1914, four days after the battle of Mons. As General Smith-Dorrien has himself broken silence after two and a half years regarding this costly battle, it is perhaps permissible for a layman, who makes no pretence of being a military expert, to examine and analyse his explanation.

It is no secret that great and controversial issues are associated with the battle of Le Cateau. The main point can be concisely stated. General Smith-Dorrien acknowledges that he fought the battle on his own responsibility, and in disregard of the repeated orders of Lord French, his Commander-in-Chief. His principal reason was, he says, that his men were too tired to retreat further. He therefore engaged them against an immensely superior force at seven o'clock in the morning. By two o'clock in the afternoon he had suffered very heavy casualties and had lost forty guns in one division alone. Thereupon he gave the order for a general retirement, which was made in some confusion.

If General Smith-Dorrien's Corps was too tired to retreat at 7 a.m. or earlier, what must its physical condition have been after fighting a seven-hours' battle against overwhelming odds and sustaining an unquestioned defeat? Was he right to disregard the most peremptory orders of the Commander-in-Chief? Did his stand near Le Cateau secure any definite advantage for the retreating Allied forces? Did he not rather imperil the concerted plans of Marshal Joffre and his own chief by risking the destruction of the Allied left? These are the principal problems of the battle of Le Cateau.

It is common ground that Lord French, after beginning the retreat from Mons, at first intended, if possible, to occupy new positions on a line extending from the direction of Cambrai, through Le Cateau, to Landrecies, on the Sambre. He says so in his despatch, but by about noon on August 25 he had come to the conclusion that he must continue the retreat in conformity with the French retirement. His left flank, in charge of General Smith-Dorrien, was exposed, and the enemy showed a tendency to envelop him.

There was a further reason for this decision of the Commander-in-Chief. The Second Corps (Smith-Dorrien's) and the First Corps (Haig's) had lost touch. By August 25 the great forest of Mormal lay between the two halves of the British Army. It is said that the intention was that the First Corps should follow the direct road west of the forest. As a matter of fact, it marched by roads to the east of the forest, and thus a great gap was left. The causes of this choice of roads by the First Corps are a subject of controversy into which I need not enter here.

On the other hand, the Second Army Corps was "well in place by evening" on the 25th, on the Le Cateau-Cambrai line. This is the evidence of the brave American Frederick Coleman whose book contains a letter from General Smith-Dorrien affirming that he was an eye-witness. Mr. Coleman seems to fix the hour at which General Smith-Dorrien was told he must retire and not fight as being seven o'clock on the evening of August 25. I think it may have been at an even earlier hour. Some time in the afternoon of the 25th General Headquarters moved from Le Cateau to St. Quentin, but the Chief of the Staff, Sir Archibald Murray, remained behind at Le Cateau. He saw General Smith-Dorrien personally and gave him his orders.

\* \* \* \*

Let us now take General Smith-Dorrien's reasons, as stated by himself, for disregarding instructions. His first plea, that his men were too tired to march further, has been already mentioned. But what are the facts? Some of the units of the Second Corps seem to have been in their new positions on the Le Cateau line quite early on August 25. I turn again to the evidence of Mr. Coleman, who took Lieutenant-Colonel Lord Loch from Le Cateau to Reumont, **the headquarters of Sir Charles Fergusson's 5th Division, " before noontide" on the 25th.** Reumont is well behind the Le Cateau line. Mr. Coleman says:

> The evidence of my eyes discredited the stories in which the 5th Division troops had been described to me as badly hammered. The infantry seemed in good shape, except for tired feet, and the artillery, horses and men, in fine fettle.

Be it marked again that this was before noon on the 25th. There are other confirmatory details, such as "a battalion of Jocks" coming into Bertry, General Smith-Dorrien's headquarters, "in mid-afternoon." I have heard independent testimony of the comparatively early arrival of the artillery. The 3rd Division was later, having to march five miles farther than the 5th. Certain units possibly arrived after dark. Sir Arthur Conan Doyle, for example, says that the 7th Brigade (McCracken's) was attacked in the evening near Solesmes, and did not reach its battle position at Caudry until after midnight; but he also considers that the heads of the columns of the Second Corps did not arrive at the Le Cateau position until 3 p.m. on the 25th, which is in conflict with other testimony. On the whole, and with limited exceptions, Mr. Coleman probably correctly sums up the situation as it presented itself towards sunset on August 25, when he says:

> The Second Army Corps was well in place by evening. Some of the brigades were in the towns, some in camp in the fields, the rest going into position along the roads as fast as they arrived. The first battalions were divided into working parties, and while trenches were being dug kettles were singing merrily over roadside fires.

The most authoritative witness of all is Lord French, who says that *" by about 6 p.m.* [on the 25th] *the Second Corps had got into position."*

\* \* \* \*

Moreover during that evening and during the night of the 25th the Second Corps does not appear to have been attacked at all, save only the 7th Brigade at Solesmes. **The corps had faced far heavier attacks on the preceding days than Sir Douglas Haig and the First Corps, but had hardly marched so far.** The enemy were pounding after Haig in lorries and motor-cars, and he was heavily attacked during the night of the 25th at Landrecies and Marvilles; yet the Guards Brigade (the 4th) marched out of Landrecies at 3·30 a.m. on the 26th, and the whole First Corps was obediently continuing its retreat under Haig soon after daybreak on that day. Why did not General Smith-Dorrien do likewise?

Yet another point. Some of the troops with which General Smith-Dorrien fought the battle of Le Cateau were comparatively fresh and not battle-worn. The 4th Division, under General Snow, had begun to arrive at Le Cateau from England so early as the morning of the 23rd. It had advanced northward very early on the 25th to cover the retreat of the Second Corps, but was back in its battle position in good time on that day. General Smith-Dorrien appears to imply that he assumed control of the 4th Division without orders in an emergency. This is obviously not the case. Lord French's despatch says: "The 4th Division was placed under the orders of the General Officer Commanding the Second Army Corps." Why General Smith-Dorrien is so constantly anxious to reveal himself as acting without orders, or in violation of orders, passes the lay understanding.

If, as seems fairly certain, the Second Corps was able to obtain at least as much rest after dark on August 25 as Sir Douglas Haig's wearied and harassed troops on the other side of the Forest of Mormal, what was really the chief compelling reason which induced General Smith-Dorrien to insist upon standing fast and fighting the battle of Le Cateau?

We seem to get nearer the heart of the mystery when we read the general's words: "*And also I considered that to show our teeth was the only way of stopping the enemy.*" But it was surely no part of General Smith-Dorrien's functions to "consider" any such thing? He was simply a corps commander.

---

### "WHY I STOOD AT LE CATEAU."
#### —*General Sir H. SMITH-DORRIEN.*

I had received orders from Sir John French not to make a stand at Le Cateau but to continue retiring. These orders I could not see my way to obey, for I feared, with the men tired as they were, further retirement might end in a rout, and also I considered that to show our teeth was the only way of stopping the enemy.

I therefore informed the Commander-in-Chief by telephone of my decision. <u>I said that before I could retire I must fight and that in order to avoid a disaster a hard blow must be dealt the Germans.</u>

In reply I was informed that I was risking a Sedan. I said that I was prepared to take that risk, and it was suggested to me that Sir John might be willing to come and take over the command. But I was anxious not to avoid the responsibility. I thought if there was going to be a Sedan that, for the sake of the cause of the Allies, Sir John should be able to return to England and organise a new Army.

—*Last Sunday's " Weekly Dispatch."*

He was taking part in an immense movement which depended for its success on the strict conformity of all the units concerned throughout the Allied northern front. Surely his duty was to obey orders? According to Mr. Coleman, Sir Archibald Murray, the Chief of Staff, had told him that the orders were definite *and in writing.*" Why should the corps commander have opposed his views to those of the Commander-in-Chief?

We begin to see what Lord Ernest Hamilton presumably meant when he wrote in his book, "The First Seven Divisions," that "the main factor in deciding that Briton and German should cross swords at Le Cateau, was the primitive impulse—always strong in the Anglo-Saxon breed—to face an ugly crisis and die fighting." I suggest that a general in possession of explicit written orders twelve hours or more before the battle began should not have yielded to an impulse to disobey them, however primitive the impulse may have been.

General Smith-Dorrien says he informed the Commander-in-Chief by telephone " of my decision." Was it his duty to decide? His duty was to obey orders. He seems to have acted instead almost as though he was holding an independent command. He telephoned that " in order to avoid a disaster a hard blow must be dealt at the Germans." In reply, he says, " I was informed that I was risking a Sedan. I said that I was prepared to take that risk." He adds that " personally I had fears that there might be a Sedan." Then, in

---

### "SMITH-DORRIEN SAVED US."

—*Sir HENRY NEWBOLT.*

He (Sir Horace Smith-Dorrien) saved us in our greatest danger by being simply himself. We shall always read the history of those black days happily, because they are not a tale of hesitation or passive acceptance of disaster, but an example of how, by decision, by initiative, and by determination, drawn from the stores of his own past, a commander may turn to-day's defeat into to-morrow's victory.

On . . . the 27th the troops reached Ham. The retreat was not over, but the danger point was past.

—" *Tales of the Great War.*"

---

view of his fears, why did he act as he did when he knew that there was a gap of eight miles between his right and the nearest units of the First Corps?

It is not easy to write with respectful restraint about these admissions of a gallant and distinguished soldier. It was clearly not enough for General Smith-Dorrien to say that he was "prepared to take that risk" and that he was "anxious not to avoid the responsibility." The man who had to take the risks, who had to shoulder the responsibility, who would have had to bear the blame if half his Army had been annihilated, was the Commander-in-Chief. No corps commander, acting without regard to repeated orders, could relieve Lord French of his supreme and sole responsibility for the conduct of the operations.

\* \* \* \*

General Smith-Dorrien further says that "it was suggested to me that Sir John might be willing to come and take over the command." I have heard that this is a misunderstanding, possibly due to the telephone. According to Mr. Coleman, the officer at General Headquarters at St. Quentin, who conveyed by telephone one at least of Lord French's frequent orders to General Smith-Dorrien, was General Sir Henry Wilson, then the Sub-Chief of Staff, now with the British Mission in Russia. It was General Wilson who telephoned that Lord French "is of the opinion that in not falling back you are risking a Sedan." It seems unlikely that General Wilson could ever have suggested that Lord French would take over a corps command at so grave a moment.

But this supposed proposal by Lord French to come and take over General Smith-Dorrien's corps command has led the general to make a surprising statement. He says: "I thought if there was going to be a Sedan that, for the sake of the cause of the Allies, Sir John should be able to return to England and organise a new Army." But again one must say that it was not the business of General Smith-Dorrien to think of these extraneous matters at such a moment, or at any moment. What on earth had Lord French got to do with organising new armies? Lord Kitchener was in England. Lord Kitchener was at that moment stamping new armies out of the ground. His first call for recruits had been issued twenty days earlier, on August 7.

In his account of the beginning of the battle General Smith-Dorrien says:

> My only hope was to hold on until nightfall. *But I never expected to do so,* because we had had no time to construct trenches of any value. The ground was very open, and *both of my flanks were in the air.*

Again one asks in bewilderment why he gave battle under such impossible conditions, while the Commander-in-Chief was incessantly ordering him to withdraw? He had said that his purpose was to deal the Germans "a hard blow" in order "to avoid a disaster." One would rather say that rarely has there been such an invitation to disaster.

The battle of Le Cateau was no disaster and for this General Smith-Dorrien deserves full credit. It is generally admitted that he showed great skill and coolness in extricating his badly hammered forces when he broke off the battle early in the afternoon. But Le Cateau greatly marred the success of the retreat from Mons, and it was responsible for a very large proportion of the total casualties suffered by the British Army during the period from the battle of Mons to the battle of the Marne.* The whole of the operations from Mons to the Marne cost us from 16,000 to 18,000 men. Nearly 10,000 of these casualties were sustained at Le Cateau, where also we lost most of the guns destroyed during the retreat. Is it surprising, therefore, that the reasons for fighting this battle should be closely scrutinised now that they have been disclosed by General Smith-Dorrien?

Sir Arthur Conan Doyle estimates that the British forces which fought at Le Cateau numbered 70,000 men; but that is "putting every unit at its full complement," and the real total in action was appreciably less. We had 225 guns. The enemy numbered 170,000, "with an overpowering artillery." Lord Ernest Hamilton says:

> The battle of Le Cateau was in the main an artillery duel, and a very unequal one at that. The afternoon infantry attack was only sustained by certain devoted regiments who failed to interpret with sufficient readiness the order to retire. Some of these regiments—as the price of their ignorance of how to turn their backs to the foe—were all but annihilated. But this is a late story. Up to midday the battle was a mere artillery duel. Our infantry lined their inadequate trenches and were bombarded for some half a dozen hours on end. Our artillery replied with inconceivable heroism, but they were outnumbered by at least five to one. . . By the afternoon many of our batteries had been silenced, and the German gunners had it more or less their own way.

The same writer says, however, that when the German infantry massed for the attack their losses from our shrapnel "must have been enormous." Lord French says in his despatch that although our artillery were outmatched "by at least four to one," they "made a splendid fight, and inflicted heavy losses on the foe." Yet the end was certain before the battle began. The German infantry began to work round into the gap on General Smith-Dorrien's right, while also pressing hard on his left flank. He himself acknowledges that he heard, between one and two o'clock, that the 5th Division, on the right, was being "knocked to pieces by the German artillery," and that "the men could not hold out any longer." He then gave the order for the whole force to retire, and when the 5th Division began to move "a great number of battalions" were "in a great state of disorder." The only marvel is that these gallant regiments stood so long.

\* \* \* \*

No one doubts that officers and men alike who fought that day won imperishable glory. There were innumerable deeds of personal heroism. Yate charging with his handful of Yorkshires, Reynolds rescuing the guns, and many like episodes, can never be forgotten. But the cost was high. Hunter-Weston's Brigade, part of Snow's Division on the left, lost 30 officers and 1,115 men. The 12th Brigade, also on the left, had 1,000 casualties. On the right the 2nd Battalion King's Own Yorkshire Light Infantry lost 20 officers and 600 men. The 1st Gordon Highlanders were almost annihilated, losing 80 per cent. killed, wounded, and missing. The 2nd Royal Scots had 400 casualties. Various other battalions suffered severely.

Was the battle worth the price paid? Did the stand at Le Cateau fulfil any useful object? Was General Smith-Dorrien justified in disregarding his orders? Did he really deal "a hard blow"?

Until the evidence is far more carefully sifted than is possible at present there will always be doubts in many minds on these points. Personally I have still to learn of any soldier of eminence who approves of General Smith-Dorrien's decision to give battle at Le Cateau or of his strange repudiation of the behests of his Commander-in-Chief.

The strongest point made in General Smith-Dorrien's favour is that after the battle the enemy did not pursue with any vigour. They had got into the gap between the two halves of the British Army, but they never drove their thrust home, as General Foch struck through the gap in the German line at the Marne. The suggestion is that the Germans had suffered too heavily at the battle of Le Cateau to follow up their advantage.

A more probable explanation is that the enemy were deterred by the fierce attacks of General Sordet's cavalry on their right flank late in the afternoon, when the battle was at an end. Sordet had 15,000 French horse, and beyond him General d'Amade's army was hurrying up from Arras. Lord French's **despatch says that Sordet did not come into action until August 27, but this is wrong.** Sordet was spurring hard for the field on the afternoon of the 26th, and it was probably the menace he and d'Amade were offering which saved the Second British Corps from pursuit. The date of Lord French's despatch shows that it must have been **hurriedly written at the time of the battle of the Marne, and doubtless full reports had not been received. It may be hoped that future chroniclers will do justice to General Sordet and his cavalry.**

Students of this remarkable battle may ask why Lord French did not himself hurry to the Le Cateau front on the morning of the battle, in order to insist upon General Smith-Dorrien's acquiescence in his orders, so often repeated, so invariably flouted. I believe the answer will be found to be that the Commander-in-Chief was summoned on the morning of the 26th to a conference of crucial importance with Marshal Joffre, whose plans were being modified and developed from day to day in accordance with changing conditions. It is said that the moment the conference was over Lord French sprang into his car and hurried towards Le Cateau. The road was blocked with fugitives from Maubeuge, progress was difficult, and before half the distance was covered a message arrived that General Smith-Dorrien had broken off the battle and was retiring.

Yet if General Smith-Dorrien was wrong in fighting the battle of Le Cateau, then Lord French made one unfortunate mistake. He ought not to have shielded his subordinate as he did in his first despatch. **It was a chivalrous thing** to do, it was in accordance with the past traditions of our Army, but it was an error. Such errors have been committed again and again in this war, and we have always had to pay dearly for them in the end. Had Lord French confined himself to praising General Smith-Dorrien for extricating the bulk of his forces at the end of the battle he would have been on safe ground; but if the battle ought never to have been fought then the country should have been told.

Was General Smith-Dorrien right or wrong? I have stated my personal view, but history must finally decide.

# APPENDIX D.

## LOSSES SUFFERED IN MONS SALIENT BY 8TH AND 9TH INF. BRIGADES.

### EXTRACT FROM G.S. DIARY OF 3RD DIVISION.

"23RD AUGUST, 1914.

".... German attack developed against the right of 9th Brigade and left of 8th Bde. (where our positions formed a pronounced salient) about 11 a.m.

"Coming on in considerable force against our weakly held line, they broke through about 2 p.m.

"In consequence of the enemy having crossed the Canal at several points, the Division was withdrawn to a previously selected position which included the hill at BOIS LA HAUT, and ran west past CUESMES ....

"They (the Germans) crossed the Canal in considerable strength between the 3rd Division and 5th Divn. and appeared to be working round our (3rd Division) left flank."

### FIELD MESSAGES FROM THE 3RD DIV.
### APPENDICES TO G.S. DIARY.

(App. X.)

TO 3RD DIV. 51. 23rd Aug.

Commdg. Middlesex reports as follows:—

My picquet on OBOURG STATION and No. 5 LOCK driven in 12·50 p.m.

From 8th Bde. 1·9 p.m. (Received 1·20 p.m.)

(Sent on as G. 122 to II. Corps, and received 1·43 p.m.)

---

TO 3RD DIVISION.

Royal Fusiliers have six battalions deployed against them, they are now retiring. There are no troops in CUESMES, can a reserve be sent there.

FROM Lieut. Harte. HANDED IN 1·42 p.m. (Received 1·45 p.m.)

---

TO 3RD DIVISION. 59. 23rd August.

Middlesex and Royal Irish on my left flank are suffering heavily. Germans are over Canal. I have no further reinforcements and they are necessary on this flank.

FROM 8th Inf. Bde. 2·15 p.m. (Received 2·25 p.m.)

TO II. CORPS. 128. 23rd August.

All reports go to show that enemy's main attack is against the MONS Salient. The troops there are suffering casualties and enemy have crossed the Canal.

My 7th Bde. is occupying the position I indicated. I have no troops available to further strengthen the BOIS LA HAUT locality.

FROM 3rd Division. 2·35 p.m. (Sd.) E. R.

---

FROM II. CORPS MESSAGE FILE.

To II. Corps. G. 127. 23rd August.

In reply to No. G. 248 received. Penetration of Outpost line necessitates withdrawal (to) main defensive position south of MONS.

From 3rd Division. 1·23 p.m. (2·23 p.m. ?) (Received 3·36 p.m.)

G. 248 ran as follows :—

TO 3RD DIVISION. G. 248. 23rd August.

Reference your G. 122 does retirement from OBOURG STATION entail any further retirement. Have any bridges in that neighbourhood been destroyed. Message just received from C.-in-C. lays stress on importance of retaining MONS.

From II. Corps. 1·50 p.m. (sd.) F. G. HARDY, Lt.-Col. G.S.

To II. Corps. G. 129. 23rd August. Situation at 3 p.m.

Royal Fusiliers are retiring through MONS, Royal Irish and Middx. are heavily engaged about FAUGB. LAZARE N. of MONS and are being pressed back. Our mounted troops have been driven in from VILLERS S. GHISLAIN. 8th Brigade are reported to be running short of ammunition.

FROM 3rd Division 3·50 p.m. (Sd.) E. R.

---

TO 5TH DIVISION. G. 131. 23rd August. In reply to No. G. 109.

Enemy are across Canal north of MONS am withdrawing my line . . . Enemy's main attack is being delivered on MONS from the direction of OBOURG and MAISLERES.

FROM 3rd Division. 4·8 p.m.

---

To II. Corps. G. 138. 23rd August.

Royal Scots Fusiliers have been attacked in flank from FLENU and pushed back from FRAMERIES road .

From 3rd Division. 6·15 p.m.

## APPENDIX E.

[COPY]

Confidential Memorandum
 For the Secretary of State for War.

 Explaining the circumstances which led up to the moment on the 6th May, 1915, when General Sir H. L. Smith-Dorrien came to the conclusion that the only patriotic course for him to take was to request the C.-in-C. of the British Forces in France to appoint a new Commander to the 2nd Army.

———

Red Lion Hotel,
Henley-on-Thames,
My dear Lord Kitchener, 14-5-15.

 I think on the whole I had better send you a copy of the ONLY communication I have had from Sir J. French—with reference to my resignation, as it makes the memorandum I prepared for you on the subject quite complete. Sir J's letter was written after the memorandum and received by me in England on the 10th May.

 It is evident from the tone of his letter that he imputes no blame to me, that his wish is to suppress the fact that I resigned, whilst implying that the campaign had affected my nerves and health so seriously as to make rest imperative. I conclude that the latter is the explanation he will allow to get about of my disappearance from the Field Army. Any comments on my part are unnecessary, for it is obvious that he cannot have chosen this course in my interests.

 Unfortunately, I am the only General in high command from the commencement of the Campaign who has not received public recognition at the hands of His Majesty—for instance, Sir J. himself received an O.M., Haig was promoted, etc., etc., and I am told that the conclusion then drawn was that French's glowing mention of me in his first dispatch was not accepted at its face value and as since then, whilst the Commander of the 1st Army has been constantly lauded, whilst no reference has been made to myself, people are getting confirmed in the view that I have been more or less a failure.

 Luckily, for my peace of mind, I know what H.M. and you think and that is all that concerns me.

Yours sincerely,
(Sd.) H. L. S.-D.

XXX.

Head Quarters,
British Army.

May 8, 1915.

My dear Smith-Dorrien,

The action* I have taken has resulted from the firm conviction I have that you need rest after the terrible trial and strains to which you have been subjected since August last.

I write this short line to express the deep regret I feel personally and to ask you to accept my heartfelt gratitude for the help you have given me.

Yours always sincerely,
J. D. P. FRENCH.

---

The following extract from a letter from Sir Wm. Robertson is evidence that ill-health was not the cause of my leaving Sir J. French's Command.

General Head Quarters,
British Army in the Field,
27-5-15.

My dear Sir Horace,

I certainly will do anything I can to prevent the spreading of reports that you have broken down in health, but I have never heard a whisper this side. Why should I? No one thinks so. It is a London yarn. I heard from there the other day you were in a Nursing Home! . . . . . . . . . .

Yours sincerely,
W. R. ROBERTSON.

---

## MEMORANDUM.

Lord Kitchener will remember that on the 19th August, 1914, when he told me that the King had selected me to succeed the late Sir J. Grierson, he remarked he had just been warned by the C. of S., Sir Charles Douglas, that for some time past the attitude of Sir John French to me had been a very hostile one, that the hostility was entirely on his side and that my position under him in the Army in France might be a difficult one.

---

*It is not clear what action of his Sir John French refers to. It cannot be with regard to my leaving his command for as these papers show that was entirely voluntary on my part.—H. L. S.-D.

I have reason to believe that Sir John resisted my being appointed and asked that Sir Herbert Plumer might be sent instead.

In the great retreat which commenced on the 24th August, 1914, the troops under my Command were fortunate enough to save the force from serious disaster, and for this I was given full credit in Sir John French's dispatches.

Although I incurred Sir John French's anger from time to time up to the end of the year for no apparent reason, he seems to have been sufficiently satisfied with my success as a Corps Commander to have recommended me for the command of the 2nd Army.

From this time on, however, the attitude of the Field Marshal towards me became increasingly difficult. He blamed me for everything which did not bring him success. For the heavy sick list and casualties in the 27th and 28th Divisions in January and February he held me entirely to blame, and no arguments of mine made the smallest impression on him.

Amongst other arguments, I used the following :—

(a) The Divisions were only Divisions in name, each being formed of 12 Battalions, collected from all parts of the Empire, mostly from hot climates without any previous training in Brigade or Division, with only Territorial Auxiliary Services in the way of Field and Signal Companies R.E. and Medical Units and with Brigadiers who had never previously commanded a Brigade.

(b) That he sent these Divisions as they arrived in the country to take over from the French badly constructed trenches full of water in most poisonous weather, and in the area which was known to be held in greater strength by the enemy than any other part of their line opposite the British Army.

(c) That the attitude of Germans to British round YPRES was very different to that shown towards the French troops, and that they showed it by subjecting our troops to a continuous and vigorous offensive day and night from the moment our troops took over the trenches.

(d) That the troops had all come from hot climates and were physically quite unfit to stand life in the trenches in such rigorous weather without a very heavy sick list.

(e) If the Germans exploded a mine or captured a trench, or if a small local enterprise on one of my Brigade fronts was not completely successful, it was all my fault and yet he would argue that I did not set my mind sufficiently on the higher duties of Command of an Army, but worried too much about petty details and interfered too much with Corps Commanders. I told him, in reply, that the role he had allotted to my Army was to spread out on a large front (about three times as long as the 1st Army) with a view to holding the enemy, thus leaving me only sufficient troops for small local reserves, but that my plans for a big offensive on any part of my front were all matured and could be put into execution, whenever he gave me sufficient troops for the purpose.

I invited him to give me a few concrete examples of my shortcomings so that I might rectify them, but this he said he could not do, as he was merely telling me his impressions.

On one occasion because "I HAD ALLOWED" the Germans to open a sudden burst of Artillery fire and follow it by an infantry attack on St. Eloi on the 14th March, he personally abused me and my Army in no unmeasured terms and said he was considering whether it would be possible for us to complete the campaign together.

On the 7th April, I was informed that the 3rd Corps, except for administrative purposes, had been removed from my Army.

On the 22nd April, the whole of the left of my Army was exposed and the approach to YPRES laid open by a German onslaught, commenced by an application of gas, on French troops, and I at once set to work to restore the situation, which, thanks largely to Sir Herbert Plumer, the Commander on the spot, I succeeded in doing.

On more troops being sent by the C.-in-C. to the YPRES area for offensive action in co-operation with the French, it was suggested to me verbally by the C. of S. that it would be throwing too much on Sir H. Plumer, with only a Corps Staff, to conduct the further operations and I told him that I fully realised this and was moving myself to an Advanced Headquarters where I would personally command.

I had a personal interview with the C.-in-C. on the 25th April and received his verbal instructions, which are set forth in my letter to the Field Marshal of the 30th April, vide PAPER B.

On the morning of the 27th April, the fifth morning after the French retirement, having in view the fact that the C. of S. had written to me on the 24th April and Sir John had verbally impressed on me the next day that I should be prepared to surrender ground by taking a more retired line East of YPRES, unless the French recovered much of the ground they had lost, I thought it right to inform him that I saw little hope of the French recovering any ground and further, to make his mind easy, I remarked that I had arranged a series of retired lines, so that if it became necessary to fall back, the C.-in-C. might know there would be no difficulty about doing it, but I added "*I do not think we have arrived at the time to adopt these measures.*" The full text of the letter is enclosed—PAPER " C."

About 4 to 4·30 p.m. (the 27th) a Staff Officer arrived with a paper from the C. of S. saying the Chief considered I was taking a pessimistic view of the situation.

At 4·30 p.m., Br.-General Maurice left ST. OMER (G.H.Q.) with PAPER D, conveying instructions, *not to me but* to Sir H. Plumer telling him to consolidate the line he was holding and to prepare a line East of YPRES, for occupation if and when it became necessary to withdraw from the present salient.

This is exactly what I had told the C. of S. I was doing in my letter of that morning, PAPER C, which the Chief considered as pessimistic.

At 4·35 p.m., the following telegram IN CLEAR was sent to my Advanced Headquarters, repeated to my permanent Headquarters, and also to the 5th Corps:—

" Priority—G.H.Q. 4·44 p.m.

" To Advanced Second Army. O.A. 976. 27th.

" Chief directs you to hand over forthwith to General " Plumer the command of all troops engaged in the present " operations about YPRES. You should lend Gen. Plumer " your Br.-General General Staff and such other officers of " the various Branches of your Staff as he may require. " General Plumer should send all reports to G.H.Q., from " which he will receive his orders. Acknowledge. Addressed " 2nd Army, repeated 5th Corps.

" G.H.Q. 4·35 p.m."

This telegram must have been written after the instructions in PAPER D to Sir H. Plumer which actually left G.H.Q. in

Br.-General Maurice's hands at 4·30 p.m. vide his letter PAPER E. In other words, it is clear that the C.-in-C. instructed General Plumer to carry out the very thing I said I was doing, *i.e.*, "*Consolidating the line I was holding and preparing a line East of YPRES in case retrenchment should become necessary*" before he placed Sir H. Plumer, instead of myself, in charge of the operations.

I would remark here that had the Chief wished to satisfy himself as to the true meaning of the only sentence which could be construed as pessimistic, and this only by disregarding the whole of the remainder of the letter, it would have been perfectly simple to have asked either by wire or motor cyclist, for he received that letter about midday and it was not until 4·35 p.m. that he sent the open wire relieving me. I would further remark that he must have wished to make it impossible for me to remain in command of the 2nd Army, or he would have sent the instructions in cipher or by motor cyclist.

I have entered into these details to show that no matter what I did my actions were always misconstrued.

On the night of the 27th April, I returned to my permanent Headquarters shorn of all my Staff and all my troops, except a part of the 2nd Corps and discredited by my Chief in the eyes of a considerable number of the 2nd Army, who had seen the telegram in the several offices to which it was sent.

I recognised that this state of affairs could not go on, and on the 30th April I wrote letter "PAPER B" which I only sent on 1st May to the Field Marshal under cover of PAPER A.

I submit that nothing could have been more conciliatory than the tone of those papers.

On the 3rd May, Sir John sent his private Secretary, Lieut.-Colonel Fitzgerald, to tell me he was considering most carefully what I had written and would send me a reply, very shortly, and that the contents of my letters to him were secret between him and me.

At this time, very heavy fighting was taking place round HILL 60, and on the 5th May overwhelming the garrison by an attack with gas, the Germans captured the Hill and even a support trench in rear of it, thus penetrating my line within a few hundred yards of the point where the 5th Corps and the 2nd Corps joined. The reserves of the 2nd Corps were all being used up, and as the 5th Corps was not under my orders I could not employ troops of that Corps to restore the situation.

xxxv.

Early on the 6th May, I received an order to attend a meeting of Army Commanders at the Chief's house next morning to confer on the subject of a strong offensive by the 1st Army, which was to commence on the 8th. Further, I had been told that the French were actually commencing a big offensive on the right of the 1st Army on the morrow (*i.e.*, the 7th)

Now, all experiences of our taking offensive action against any part of the enemy's line had taught us that they would retaliate by a vigorous offensive against another part of our line.

"For example, the attack on ST. ELOI whilst the 1st Army was attacking NEUVE CHAPELLE," and fearing that the lack of control of the 2nd Army under one Commander in the neighbourhood of HILL 60 might spell disaster if the Germans attacked there in the next few days, I came to the conclusion that the only patriotic step for me to take was to sacrifice myself, and I accordingly wrote the following letter to Sir John French which was delivered to his A.D.C. on duty at 9˙15 a.m. on the 6th May, 1915 :—

"6th May, 1915.

"My dear Field Marshal,

"I have just received an order for Army Commanders to "meet at your house at 9 a.m. to-morrow. I am still in "ignorance of the action you intend to take regarding the "papers, so important to me and the Army I command, I "sent you on the 1st instant, and it would make things easier "for me, were I to know your views before the meeting.

"Whatever may be the reason, there can be no question "that your attitude to me for some time past has been to "show that you had, for some reason or other unknown to "me, ceased to trust me.

"Latterly, I have been shorn first of one wing of my Army "and then of the other, on the latter occasion the announce-"ment being made in such a way and in such terms, as "to leave no doubt in the minds of many in the 2nd Army "that their Commander was no longer believed in by their "Chief.

"My position as Army Commander has become impossible "and I regard my remaining in Command, with a cloud hang-"ing over me ready to burst at any moment, as a positive "danger to the cause for which we are fighting.

"Plenty of complicated situations have arisen in the last few months, and the difficulty of dealing with them has been greatly enhanced by the knowledge that unless I was successful, I and the 2nd Army would be blamed—*in fact I have had more to fear from the rear than from the front.*

"We have got to win this War and to do so there must be no weak links in the chain. Your attitude to me constitutes a very seriously weak link, and I feel sure, that trying as that attitude has been to me, you have not wished to carry it quite so far as to appoint someone else to command the 2nd Army in my place.

"This step is, however, the only one which to my mind will strengthen up the chain again, and it is to render it more easy for you to take it without further delay that I am writing this letter.

"Please do not let any false considerations for me personally stand in the way, for the War Office will doubtless find some place for me where I can still do useful work towards helping our Army fighting in France.

"Yours sincerely,

"(Sd.) H. L. SMITH-DORRIEN."

---

I again received no reply from the Field Marshal, but at 7·30 p.m. that evening (the 6th May) I received the following official from his Adjutant General:—

"General Sir H. Smith-Dorrien, G.C.B.,
"Commanding II Army.

"The C.-in-C. directs me to inform you that the Secretary of State for War wishes to see you, and he requests that you will proceed to England to-morrow—7th May—Lieut.-General Sir H. Plumer has been instructed to assume Command of the II Army and informed that you will communicate direct with him, as to when you leave for England. Kindly arrange this together with any information you may consider it necessary to give him. Please acknowledge receipt of this memo.

"(Sd.) C. F. N. MACREADY, A.G.

"G.H.Q. 6-5-15."

I am not asking for any redress, for, of course, a C.-in-C. of an Army in the Field must be omnipotent, and must be given a free hand in the selection of the tools he has to work with, but I owe it you as the Secretary of State for War who advised His Majesty to appoint me to the Command of the 2nd Army of the Expeditionary Force, to explain what has happened, and I submit that in the interest of the Cause for which we are fighting I have made it clear that the only course left open to me was to ask to be relieved of a Command, my retention of which, for reasons known only to himself, appeared to be increasing the difficulties of Field Marshal Sir John French in conducting this arduous campaign.

(Sd.) H. L. SMITH-DORRIEN,
General.

7th May, 1915.

## PAPER " A."

1st May, 1915.

My dear Field Marshal,

There is nothing in the least urgent in these papers but will you as an old friend of many years find 5 minutes in the next day or two to read them through. The telegram removing me from the Command of the operations round YPRES was sent "in clear" to Advanced 2nd Army at HAZEBROUCK, so many in the 2nd Army are aware that you are not satisfied with their Commander and I owe it to my Army to explain matters with a view to regaining your confidence.

I have put it in writing as I thought it would take less of your time to read my explanation, than if I gave it personally.

Yours sincerely,

(Sd.) H. L. SMITH-DORRIEN.

---

## PAPER " B."

[COPY]

30th April, 1915.

My dear Field Marshal,

It has been due to my wish to avoid troubling you on a personal matter whilst your mind was so occupied by this disappointing upset to your plans by the retirement of the French, that I have waited to write this letter to you.

You have always given me credit for loyally trying to carry out your plans, whether in S. Africa or elsewhere, and it is a great blow to me to feel that you no longer do so, and I cannot help thinking that when you know the facts, you will not only have your confidence in me restored, but will give me credit for the way I handled what I think you will admit was a by no means easy situation.

On the evening of the 25th at ST. OMER you gave me your views and instructions which were generally as follows:

"You did not want to surrender any ground if it could "possibly be avoided, but unless the French regained the "ground they had lost, or a great deal of it, you realised that "it might become impossible to retain our present very salient "position in front of YPRES. It was essential, though, that "the situation should be cleared up, and the area quieted "down as soon as possible, even if I had to withdraw to a xxxix

"more retired line, so that you might be able to continue your "offensive elsewhere. You felt sure I should not take a re-"tired line until all hope of the French recovering ground "had vanished. You did not wish me to have many more "heavy casualties, as you thought the French had got us into "the difficulty and ought to pull us out of it.

"You mentioned that in any combined attack I was to be "careful to see that our troops did not get ahead of the "French." *

I will not trouble you with more details than I can help to explain my actions.

The disaster to the French occurred on the evening of the 22nd, by dawn on the 23rd a sort of a line of our troops had been formed across the gap made by our Allies' withdrawal. This on the curve they took up from the point where the French originally joined the Canadians to the Canal bank S. of BOESINGHE was about 8,000 yards. It was late in the morning before I could ascertain where the Germans were and directly I did, realising the importance of a second counter-attack before the Germans could make strong defences, I placed all the troops I could lay my hands on under General Plumer for the purpose, *i.e.*, my own Army Reserve consisting of a Canadian Brigade and the 13th Brigade, and I told him to use the only other available troops, namely, 7 Battalions, 27th and 28th Divisions, which were Divisional reserves.

Plumer said he could not withdraw all the latter from their proper role, but I told him he must and I made him happy later on by saying you had given me the use of the Northumbrian Division, which would be up in time to provide reserves for elsewhere.

It naturally took time to collect these troops and organise this attack, but by 4 p.m. he was able to move forward on both sides of the YPRES-PILCKEM road and took the front line of German trenches, but the French, who were to have moved forward in co-operation, did not budge.

I will not enter into the story of the next few days, but suffice it to say I was personally in close touch with the French, frequently seeing General Putz and urging him to more vigorous offensive, and on the morning of the 27th I at last came to the conclusion that any chance of the French wresting back lost ground was very remote indeed.

---

\* This last instruction was also conveyed to me written at 10 a.m. on 26th from C.G S. as follows :—" Attack same time as French. Secretly keep in "mind not to attack before them."

Accordingly, I wrote to Robertson a statement of the situation for your information.

I have gathered from Robertson that the view you took of my letter was that I had no confidence in being able to carry out my plans, and that you had come to the conclusion through one unfortunate phrase which appears to have given a totally different impression to what was intended.

The phrase reads :—

"I intend to-night if nothing special happens to reorganise "the new front and to withdraw superfluous troops West of "YPRES."

The new front I referred to was the one our advanced troops were fighting on when I wrote, where the units were rather mixed. By "superfluous troops" I referred chiefly to exhausted units. I had, as a matter of fact, too many troops East of YPRES, except for weighty offence and as units were getting exhausted and I had arranged to co-operate with the French in a fresh attack that afternoon (the 27th) I knew they would be more exhausted still, and that rest in the fire-swept area E. of YPRES being impossible, the only thing to do was to withdraw them West.

The attack was to be made by the weakened Lahore Division next to the French, with the 10th Brigade on their right, Plumer's Corps Reserve of 4 Battalions supporting the former, and the 13th and Northumberland Brigades the latter.

On ST. JULIEN itself, and to the East of it, I did not think it advisable to ADVANCE to the attack, for until ground had been gained towards the line PILCKEM-FORTUIN an advance on that front would merely accentuate the salient and entail loss without any advantage.

Robertson told me that your interpretation of the phrase was that I was already starting that night, thinning out my advanced troops with a view to retirement as in a rearguard action. Directly he pointed this out to me, I saw that such a meaning could perfectly well be understood from it, but I can assure you that nothing was further from my mind than any thought of retirement, and this is borne out by a sentence a few lines previous in that same letter, which reads:—

"I think it right to put these views before the Chief, but make "it clear that although I am preparing for the worst I do not "think we have arrived at the time when it is necessary to adopt "these measures."

With regard to pessimism I cannot detect any in that letter with regard to OUR troops. I see I talk of "heavy fighting "with fairly satisfactory results and very heavy losses to the "enemy."

The letter, however, is full of justifiable pessimism regarding the chances of the French gaining ground.

Remember—you had impressed on me that unless they gained sufficient ground I must be prepared to relinquish some of ours, and there they were, the 5th morning after the disaster, frittering away their troops in small futile attacks, in which they had certainly never gained a yard, and from the orders for their fresh attack that afternoon I was convinced that nothing further would result that day.

With regard to there being any doubt in my mind as to my ability to carry out my plans, I submit that my letter showed that I was prepared for any eventuality and it was to set your mind at rest that I entered into particulars.

Except from the impressions you got from my badly-expressed letter to Robertson that I was actually commencing to retire, I submit you were generally in accord with what I did.

For instance—The use of the Cavalry to watch in case the Germans broke through North of the French. Directly I heard you were sending the Cavalry, I asked that a Division might be sent there and when you put the Corps under my orders I at once requested Byng to take that as his principal role, and when the French said it was unnecessary I persuaded Putz it was necessary, and to get my way placed Byng under Putz for the purpose until such time as sufficient French reinforcements arrived to safeguard that flank. I subsequently received a note from Robertson that you thought the Cavalry should be employed there.

Then, with regard to my plan in case of retirement, I gather if such becomes necessary, Plumer is adopting my plan more or less, and that you have approved of it and so it can only have been that wretchedly-expressed phrase which gave you the impression that I was actually off and which decided you to take no risks.

In a war such as this, there is no room for taking risks, but I trust now I have explained matters, you will send for me and tell me that so far from deserving blame I did not handle the situation too badly after all.

Yours sincerely,

(Sd.) H. L. Smith-Dorrien.

**PAPER "C."**

SECRET.

[COPY]

Advanced Headquarters, 2nd Army,
27th April, 1915.

My dear Robertson,

In order to put the situation before the Commander-in-Chief, I propose to enter into a certain amount of detail.

You will remember that I told Colonel Montgomery the night before last, after seeing General Putz's orders, that as he was only putting in a small proportion of his troops (and those at different points) to the actual attack, I did not anticipate any great results. You know what happened—the French right, instead of gaining ground, lost it, and the left of the Lahore Division did the same, but the British Regiment on the right of the Lahore Division, the Manchesters, did very well and took some enemy trenches and held them for a considerable time.

The Northumberland Brigade to their right made a very fine attack on ST. JULIEN and got into it, but were unable to remain there.

Away to the right, between ST. JULIEN and our old trenches about Square D. 10, there was a good deal of fighting, but with fairly satisfactory results—the Germans eventually retiring.

*The enemy's losses are very heavy. Artillery Observing Officers claim to have mown them down over and over again during the day.* At times, the fighting appears to have been heavy, and our casualties are by no means slight.

I enclosed you on a separate paper the description of the Line the troops are on at this moment. I saw General Putz last night about to-day's operations, and he told me he intended to resume the offensive with very great vigour. I saw his orders, in which he claims to have captured HET SAS, but on my asking him what he meant he said the houses of that place which are to the West of the Canal. He told me also that the success at LIZERNE had been practically nil—in fact, that the Germans were still in possession of the village or were last night.

From General Putz's orders for to-day, he is sending one Brigade to cross the River East of BRIELEN to carry forward the troops on the East of the Canal in the direction of PILCKEM, and he assured me that this Brigade was going to be pushed in with **great** vigour.

It was not till afterwards that I noticed that, to form his own reserve, he is withdrawing two Battalions from the East of the Canal and another two Battalions from the front line in the same part to be used as a reserve on that bank of the River, so the net result of his orders is to send over six fresh Battalions to the fighting line and to withdraw four which had already been employed.

I have lately received General Joppé's orders. He is the General Commanding the attack towards PILCKEM on the East of the Canal, and I was horrified to see that he, instead of using the whole of this Brigade across the Canal for this offensive, is leaving one Regiment back at BRIELEN, and only putting the other Regiment across the Canal to attack—so the net result of these latter orders with regard to the strength of the troops on the East of the Canal for the fresh offensive is the addition of one Battalion.

I need hardly say that I at once represented the matter pretty strongly to General Putz, but I want the Chief to know this as I do not think he must expect that the French are going to do anything very great—in fact, although I have ordered the Lahore Division to co-operate when the French attack, at 1˙15 p.m., I am pretty sure that our line to-night will not be in advance of where it is at the present moment.

I fear the Lahore Division have had very heavy casualties, and so they tell me have the Northumbrians, and I am doubtful if it is worth losing any more men to regain this French ground unless the French do something really big.

Now, if you look at the map, you will see that the line the French and ourselves are now on allows the Germans to approach so close with their guns that the area East of YPRES will be very difficult to hold, chiefly because the roads approaching it from the West are swept by shell fire, and were all yesterday, and are being to-day. Again, they are now able to shell this place, POPERINGHE, and have done it for the last three days; all day yesterday at intervals there were shells close to my Report Centre and splinters of one struck the house opposite in the middle of the day, and splinters of another actually struck the house itself about midnight—in other words, they will soon render this place unhealthy.

If the French are not going to make a big push, the only line we can hold permanently and have a fair chance of keeping supplied, would be the G.H.Q. line passing just East of WIELTJE and POTIJZE, with a curved switch which is being prepared through HOOGE, the centres of Squares I. 18. d., I. 24. b. and d., to join on to our present line about a thousand yards North-East of HILL 60.

This, of course, means the surrendering of a great deal of trench line, but any intermediate line, short of that, will be extremely difficult to hold, owing to the loss of the ridge to the East of ZONNEBEKE, which any withdrawal must entail.

*I think it right to put these views before the Chief, but at the same time to make it clear that, although I am preparing for the worst, I do not think we have arrived at the time when it is necessary to adopt those measures.* In any case, a withdrawal to that line in one fell swoop would be almost impossible on account of the enormous amount of guns and paraphernalia which will have to be withdrawn first, and therefore if, withdrawal becomes necessary, the first contraction would be, starting from the left, " our present line as far as the spot where the HANNEBEKE stream crosses the road at the junction of Squares D. 7 and D. 13, thence along the subsidiary line which is already prepared, as far as the South-East corner of Square J. 2, *from whence a switch has been prepared into our old line* on the East side of J. 14. b., *i.e.*, just excluding the POLYGONE WOOD." I intend to-night, if nothing special happens, to *re-organise*\* the new front and to withdraw *superfluous*† troops West of YPRES.

I always have to contemplate the possibility of the Germans gaining ground West of LIZERNE, and this, of course, would make the situation more impossible—in fact, it all comes down to this, that unless the French do something really vigorous the situation might become such as to make it impossible for us to hold any line East of YPRES.

*It is very difficult to put a subject such as this in a letter without appearing pessimistic—I am not in the least, but as an Army Commander I have of course to provide for every eventuality and I think it right to let the Chief know what is running in my mind.*

‡More British troops, of course, could restore the situation—but this I consider to be out of the question, as it would interfere with a big offensive elsewhere which is after all the crux of the situation and will do more to relieve this situation than anything else.

Since writing above, our Cavalry report that the French actually took the whole of LIZERNE last night, capturing 120 Germans, and are now attacking the bridgehead covering the bridge leading over the Canal to STEENSTRAAT.

---

\* *i.e.*, to consolidate the line I am now holding.

† The C.G.S. in his letter dated 6 p.m. 24-4-15 had remarked that the Canadians and 13th Bde. must need replacing, but I had found it impossible and determined to do it to-night if possible.

‡ Hardly the views of a small-minded pessimist.

General Putz has answered my protest and has ordered General Joppé to put in the whole of the fresh Brigade and not to leave one Regiment of it in reserve at BRIELEN. The attack is to commence at 1·15 p.m. and we are to assist with heavy artillery fire, and the Lahore Division is only to advance if they see the French troops getting on.

Our Cavalry is where it was last night, one Division West of LIZERNE, one dismounted in reserve holding G.H.Q. trenches East of YPRES, one dismounted in huts at VLAMERTINGHE.

I am still at my Advanced Headquarters in POPERINGHE. Whether I remain here to-night again I do not know, the main advantage of my being here is my close touch with General Putz and my being able to impress my views upon him.

Yours sincerely,
(Sd.) H. L. SMITH-DORRIEN.

---

**PAPER "D."**
SECRET.

C.A. 983.
P.X. 6.

Lt.-General Sir H. Plumer, K.C.B.

1. With reference to the failure of the French attack to-day, and to the Chief's instructions given you by Brig.-General Maurice, the Chief wishes you *to consolidate the line you now hold*\* so as to render it secure against attack.

2. You are also requested *to prepare a line East of YPRES joining up with the new line now held North and South of that place ready for occupation if and when it becomes advisable to withdraw from the present salient.* Please report early as to the position of the line you select for this purpose. It should be such as to avoid withdrawal from Hill 60. The necessary instructions, if any, will be sent by G.H.Q. to 2nd Corps on receipt of your report.

3. General Foch has stated that he proposes that his troops should make a main attack from West to East to-morrow across the Canal, so as to avoid the effects of the gases

---

\*Exactly what I had told G.H.Q. I had arranged for.— H. L. S.-D.

employed by the enemy to-day and favoured by the wind from the North. He has directed General Putz to communicate with you and arrange a subsidiary attack from South to North on the East side of the Canal. If this latter attack is made by the French, the Chief wishes you to co-operate with and assist them.

(Sd.) F. MAURICE, B.G.G.S.,
for Chief of the General Staff.

G.H.Q.,
27-4-1915.

## PAPER "E."

[COPY]

General Headquarters,
British Army in the Field.
7th May, 1915.

Dear Sir Horace,

O.A. 983 was dispatched from St. Omer at 4.30 p.m. on April 27th. I took the order by motor car to Sir H. Plumer at the Chateau d'Ypres. He was out at the time and I did not see him till 6.45 p.m., when I handed him the order.

Believe me,
Yours sincerely,
(Sd.) F. MAURICE.